45⁰⁰

The Illustrated Guide to
Staffordshire Salt-glazed Stoneware

The Illustrated Guides To Pottery and Porcelain

LOWESTOFT PORCELAIN
WORCESTER PORCELAIN
LIVERPOOL HERCULANEUM POTTERY
ROCKINGHAM POTTERY AND PORCELAIN
MASON'S PATENT IRONSTONE CHINA

Frontispiece. A three-gallon enamelled punch-pot showing Bacchus astride a barrel. One of the most spectacular examples, and possibly the largest, of Staffordshire salt-glazed stoneware in existence. 10 inches high. c. 1755.

The Illustrated Guide to

STAFFORDSHIRE SALT-GLAZED STONEWARE

ARNOLD R. MOUNTFORD

PRAEGER PUBLISHERS
New York · Washington

BOOKS THAT MATTER

Published in the United States of America in 1971
by Praeger Publishers, Inc.,
111 Fourth Avenue, New York, N.Y. 10003

Library of Congress Catalog Card Number: 73-151804

Printed in Great Britain

This book is dedicated to the staff of the
City Museum and Art Gallery, Stoke-on-Trent

Contents

List of Plates

COLOUR PLATES

MONOCHROME PLATES

All between pages 58 *and* 59

Preface

While every general book on English pottery includes a section on the important and highly collectable Staffordshire salt-glazed stoneware, this is the first book to be devoted to this ware.

The author, thanks to his position as Director of the renowned Museum and Art Gallery at Stoke-on-Trent, in the heart of the Staffordshire Potteries, has been able to research deeply into a subject that has previously been little more than touched upon; and he has taken full advantage of his recent excavations on the sites of several of the eighteenth century salt-glaze potteries. Thus, the large selection of new illustrations—seen here for the first time—include many showing key-pieces recently unearthed some two hundred and fifty years after being discarded by their original maker due to manufacturing faults.

Mr. Mountford is also fortunate in being able to quote from a mass of contemporary documents, including accounts and related papers. These hitherto unpublished documents have been of the greatest value in the preparation of this book and they will doubtless be of interest to succeeding generations of students and collectors of early English pottery.

The author has made the fullest use of not only the finds at local excavations and the documents referred to but also the splendid array of salt-glazed stoneware housed in the City of Stoke-on-Trent Museum and in the leading American collections. This book will therefore be of the greatest value to all who are interested in British ceramics in general and Staffordshire pottery in particular; and it must certainly be regarded as the standard work on the subject.

As editor of the *Illustrated Guide* series, I am pleased to announce that Mr. Mountford is preparing a companion volume on Staffordshire slip-ware.

Geoffrey A. Godden
General Editor

1. A superb enamelled bottle which clearly illustrates the harmony between potter and decorator. $8\frac{3}{4}$ inches high. c. 1755.

Introduction

The term stoneware is generally applied to pottery which has withstood a high oven-temperature to such a degree (1200°–1400° centigrade) that the body has vitrified and become impervious to liquids. Clay which has not been fired to this point of vitrification is usually classed as earthenware: but in accepting this definition, it should be pointed out that in certain cases the dividing line is arbitrary—as exemplified in some earthenware made in medieval times which comes near to the accepted definition of stoneware. However, this is the exception rather than the rule.

Another generalisation concerns glazing, a refractory lead-glaze being associated with earthenware whereas when a glaze was deemed necessary on European stoneware it was achieved by using salt. On earthenware, the glaze was applied directly to the pot by sprinkling, dusting, painting or dipping; but the glaze on stoneware was the result of throwing salt into a high-temperature oven. The heat caused the salt to volatilise, and the soda in the salt combined with the alumina and silica in the clay to form a thin vitreous coating on the surface of all the ware in the oven. On earthenware, the lead-glaze is invariably smooth, shiny and glassy whereas on salt-glazed stoneware the impervious outer layer has characteristic minute pitting somewhat resembling the surface texture of orange-peel.

In Germany, salt-glazed stoneware was manufactured as early as the fifteenth century, if not earlier; but it was not until the late seventeenth century that the potters of North Staffordshire, in the area known today as Stoke-on-Trent, began their experiments which led to the purely English type of salt-glazed stoneware that forms the subject of this book.

Some writers have endeavoured to claim for Staffordshire potters the distinction of having invented English stoneware; but as will be seen, this credit must belong to those of Fulham—which, with Nottingham, was another great centre of stoneware manufacture. Despite their ceramic achievements, however, neither Fulham nor Nottingham produced ware during the eighteenth century in any way comparable to the delicate finely-potted Staffordshire varieties of thin and extremely lightweight table-ware that were to compete with the more expensive and heavier porcelain.

Plain white, 'scratch-blue', enamelled, and printed salt-glazed ware, in that order of succession, was produced and manufactured by scores of

Staffordshire potters from the first to the last quarter of the eighteenth century, together with rare small-size figures of varying degrees of accomplishment.

With the advent of mould-making and slip-casting (where liquid clay is poured into absorbent plaster-of-Paris moulds), complicated shapes no longer presented a problem—and however one might decry, for example, teapots made in amusing and fanciful shapes (animal, house etc.), it has to be admitted that the process engendered originality. What makes this class of ware so popular with collectors is the very wide range of products both in useful and ornamental articles. Staffordshire salt-glaze knew no narrow bounds. Indeed, its variety is seemingly endless.

Perhaps the most vexing aspect of collecting salt-glazed stoneware is the utter lack of factory-marked examples. Due to this, it is only on rare occasions that it is possible to link pot with potter. Recent excavations in Stoke-on-Trent have added greatly to our knowledge, and contemporary documents (published here for the first time) have provided important information; but despite this, in the majority of cases the question of attribution will remain unsolved. However, this should not dissuade the would-be collector from entering the field. Though robbed of this background detail, so many salt-glazed examples stand by themselves as works of art.

During the third quarter of the eighteenth century, there was a marked decline in the quantity of Staffordshire stoneware leaving the Potteries. It had nothing to do with recession in trade or competition from an outside source. Quite simply, another class of ware was taking its place in the kitchens and dining rooms of England. The new fashion was creamware which, though basically the same body as salt-glazed stoneware, was twice-fired at lower oven temperatures—the second firing fixing a smooth lead glaze to the surface of the ware. When, in about 1765, Josiah Wedgwood secured the patronage of Queen Charlotte and called his creamware 'Queen's Ware', it was only a matter of time before his contemporaries, conscious of his unqualified success, abandoned the old method of glazing. Gradually, as the demand for cream-coloured earthenware grew, salt-glazed stoneware was superseded. If the technique lingered on here and there in Staffordshire into the early years of the nineteenth century, it was only to supply the cheaper type of product.

When the Staffordshire potters reverted to lead-glazing during the second half of the eighteenth century, it did not signify the end of English salt-glazed stoneware. In Fulham, Lambeth and elsewhere the tradition continued by way of brown stoneware. Brampton, Denby, Belper and Chesterfield all had potters making brown salt-glazed stoneware during the second half of the eighteenth century and throughout the nineteenth century, some firms continuing into the present century. But outside Staffordshire, the process was reserved for beer-jugs, tankards, flasks and industrial ware, and the Derbyshire factories specialised in ink, blacking and furniture-paste bottles.

Fortunately, through the efforts of the Lambeth School of Art, admirably supported by Doulton's of Lambeth, there emerged a revival of decorative brown salt-glazed stoneware from the 1870s onward. Imbued with some of the feeling expressed by the Arts and Crafts movement, this deep understanding of clay projected by the later Doulton artists and the Martin brothers is in a class by itself.

With the exception of Doulton's, who have until recent times continued to manufacture special items of fine decorative stoneware, elsewhere commercial salt-glazing is mainly confined to the production of drain-pipes—a far cry from the delicate white table-ware that emanated from Staffordshire more than two centuries ago and which today is prized and enjoyed by collectors all over the world.

Acknowledgments

Unless otherwise stated, illustrations are of specimens in the City Museum and Art Gallery, Stoke-on-Trent. For permission to reproduce ware housed in the United States of America, the author is grateful to the Metropolitan Museum of Art, New York; The Nelson Gallery—Atkins Museum, Kansas City; Colonial Williamsburg; Mrs. Robert D. Chellis; and Mr. David Zeitlin.

Thanks are also due to the staff of the British Ceramic Research Association, Penkhull, Stoke-on-Trent, and the City Reference Librarian and staff of the Central Library, Hanley, Stoke-on-Trent, for their assistance. Miss Rhoda Edwards of the Minet Library London Borough of Lambeth. The Keeper and staff of the Public Record Office, London.

Chapter I

Origins in Staffordshire

On the 15th January 1765, Josiah Wedgwood noted the following particulars provided by a Mr. Steel, aged eighty-four:

> White glazed ware first made by Dutchmen at Bradwall [sic] about the year 1693. The people of Burslem were then very much surprized with the smoke of the salt glaze, and ran in great numbers to see what was the matter; amongst whom Steel was one . . . The Dutchmen staid at Bradwall 7 or 8 years. Where they went he knoweth not. There was no ware made in these parts that was glazed with salt, before the Dutchmen used it with white ware. The freckled and stone wares were made after the Dutchmen were known to use salt for glazing. And brown stone ware dipt was glazed with salt as an attempt to imitate the Dutchmens white ware:

It is evident that Wedgwood was uncertain as to the truth of these claims, as will be seen from a letter written to his partner Thomas Bentley on the 19th July 1777:

> It is only about 80 years since Mr Elers was amongst us, when there was as many Potworks in Burslem as there is now, and had been for time immemorial; and the reason for Mr Elers fixing upon Staffordshire to try his experiments seems to be that the Pottery was carried on there in a much larger way, and in a more improved state, than in any other part of Great Britain. The improvements Mr Elers made in our Manufactory were precisely these: Glazing our common clays with salt which produced Pot d'Grey or Stoneware, and this after they (the two Elers) had left the country was improved into White Stone Ware by using the White Pipe Clay instead of the common clay of this Neighbourhood, and mixing with it Flint Stones calcined and reduced by pounding into a fine powder . . . I make no doubt but glazing with salt, by casting it amongst the ware whilst it is red hot, came to us from Germany, but

whether Mr. E. was the person to whom we are indebted for this improvement I do not know.

The significance of the last sentence in relation to the introduction of salt-glazing into North Staffordshire has escaped many historians, who have perpetuated the Elers myth. If Wedgwood ever visited Bradwell, he never recorded the fact; but fortunately for us, another master potter—Enoch Wood, of Burslem—is known to have inspected the site. In 1814, he wrote:

> Report says, Salt glaze ware was made first at Bradwell about the year 1700, I have seen the foundations of the oven near the west end of the barn about 20 years since and believe it was built to fire Red China only.

This opinion was supported by John Mountford, who demolished the remains of the oven in about 1802, when he stated 'the height was about seven feet, but not like the salt glaze ovens'. In his *History of the Staffordshire Potteries*, published in 1829, Simeon Shaw wrote:

> The Oven itself had five mouths, but neither holes over the inside flues or bags, to receive the salt, had been used by them, nor scaffold on which the person might stand to throw it in . . . E. Wood, and J. Riley, Esqrs both separately measured the inside diameter of the remains, at about five feet; while other ovens, of the same date, in Burslem, were ten or twelve feet. We may also mention, that the Salt glazed Pottery of that time, was comparatively cheap; and the oven, being fired only once each week, required to be large, to hold a quantity sufficient to cover the contingent expenses. Hence we find the ovens were large, and high, and had holes in the dome, to receive the salt cast in to effect the glazing.

The interior measurement of the Elers oven, which Enoch Wood tersely rejected as having been used for salt-glazing, had the same diameter as one excavated in 1968 by the City of Stoke-on-Trent Museum Archaeological Society on land adjoining the Albion Hotel, Hanley. This unique example, which is preserved in the grounds of the City Museum, Stoke-on-Trent, is also multi-mouthed and was used to fire lead-glazed ware during the earlier part of the eighteenth century. No foundations of a salt-glaze oven have yet been found in the Potteries; but if we are to accept the fact that they were 'large and high', then the Elers oven is automatically eliminated. A potter of Enoch Wood's experience would certainly have known the difference between those employed for 'red china' and those used for salt-glaze; the evidence at Bradwell would have been all too apparent.

As one might expect, a great deal of interest has centred around the activities of the Elers brothers during their short, mysterious stay in North Staffordshire. Claims and counter-claims have, over the years, stimulated students of ceramics to explore the area in which the Dutchmen worked; but sporadic probing around Bradwell Hall yielded limited evidence. During the late 1950s, however, a series of preliminary excavations led to the recovery

11. A unique two-quart enamelled punch-pot with a portrait of Prince Charles Edward Stuart—one of the most popular subjects for the mid-eighteenth-century decorator. $8\frac{3}{4}$ inches high. c. 1755.

of many small fragments of red ware which are now in the City Museum, Stoke-on-Trent; but no salt-glazed sherds were found.

If the Elers did not introduce into Staffordshire the technique of glazing pots with salt, then how, when and where did it begin? The writer Simeon Shaw (*History of the Staffordshire Potteries*, Hanley, 1829) asks us to believe:

> About 1680, the method of GLAZING WITH SALT, was suggested by an accident; and we give the names of the parties as delivered down by tradition. In this as in many other improvements in Pottery, a close investigation of one subject has frequently reflected fresh light upon another; something altogether unexpected has been presented to notice; and not unfrequently from an incident comparatively trivial has resulted a discovery of paramount importance. At Stanley Farm (a short mile from the small pottery of Mr Palmer, at Bagnall five miles east of Burslem) the servant of Mr Joseph Yates, was boiling, in an earthen vessel, a strong lixivium of common salt, to be used some way in curing pork; but during her temporary absence, the liquor effervesced, and some ran over the sides of the vessel, quickly causing them to become red hot; the muriatic acid decomposed the surface, and when cold, the sides, were partially glazed. Mr Palmer availed himself of the hint thus obtained, and commenced making a fresh sort—the common BROWN WARE of our day; and was soon followed by the manufacturers in Holden Lane, Greenhead, and Brown Hills; the proximity of their situation to the Salt-Wyches, affording great facility for procuring the quantity of salt required for their purposes.

Though it has been proved beyond all doubt that the Bagnall explanation is a myth because it is technically impossible, the legend persists. And students continue to seek out Stanley Farm, where the local inhabitants insist that this is where the story of Staffordshire salt-glaze began. The site of the 'small Pottery of Mr. Palmer' has yet to be located. Despite intensive search in and around the village of Bagnall, I have failed to find any brown stoneware wasters, oven-furniture or, indeed, any clue in support of this tradition.

But let us, for the moment, leave the question of Staffordshire origins and see what was happening elsewhere during the second half of the seventeenth century. The first documentary reference to stoneware occurs in a patent of 1671 granted to John Dwight of Fulham—though in answers during an earlier law-suit brought by him two witnesses stated that the elder Symon Woolters of Southampton made stoneware from about 1664 to 1669 and that the younger Symon Woolters had made the same sort of ware for Mr. Killigrew of Chelsea. Dwight was granted his patent on the 23rd April 1671 for the manufacture of 'transparent earthenware commonly known by the names of Porcelaine or China and Persian ware' and also for 'stoneware vulgarly called Cologne ware' which had 'not hitherto been wrought or made' in England. Dr. Plot, in his *History of Oxfordshire*, 1677, writes:

> Let it suffice for things of this nature that the ingenious John Dwight formerly M.A. of Christ Church College, Oxon. hath discovered the

mystery of the stone or Cologne wares (such as d'Alva bottles, jugs and noggins), heretofore made only in Germany, and also by the Dutch brought over into England in great quantities; and hath set up a manufacture of the same, which (by methods and contrivances of his own, altogether unlike those used by the Germans) in three or four years' time, he hath brought it to greater perfection . . . insomuch that the Company of Glass-sellers of London, who are the dealers for that commodity, have contracted with the inventor to buy only of his English manufacture, and refuse the foreign.

By the first patent of 1671, Dwight was granted 'the sole use for fourteen years'. Before this term had expired, he made application—in 1684—for an extension of his patent rights for a second period of fourteen years, which was also granted. Other wares specified in his patents were marbled, blue, and mouse-coloured stoneware, statuettes, and red ware teapots made of Staffordshire clay. In his *Ceramic Art of Great Britain* (Virtue & Co., London, 1878) Llewellynn Jewitt gives extracts from Dwight's notebooks (the whereabouts of which are now unknown) which have an important bearing on the links already existing between London and North Staffordshire during the second half of the seventeenth century. In one of the notebooks giving recipes from 1691 onwards are the following:

> To make a bright red Cley wth Staffordshire red Cley—Take sifted Staffordshire Cley thirty pounds. ffine dark twenty pounds. Mingle & tread.

> The fine Stone Cley. Take sifted cley sixty pounds ffine white fourteen pounds, ffine white sand sifted ten pounds. Mingle and tread.

The mention of Staffordshire clay is of particular significance.

The splendid Staffordshire slipware manufactured by the Toft family and their contemporaries from the 1670s onwards found favour and was sold in many parts of England if we are to judge from fragments of the ubiquitous trailed trellis-rim patterns which continue to be recovered from excavations. We know that the Staffordshire potters sold some of their ware in London, so it is reasonable to assume that it was through these men that John Dwight obtained supplies of 'Staffordshire red Cley'. Transporting pots and clay from the Midlands to the London market was obviously good for trade and, as business increased, more and more men from the Potteries would have been drawn to the capital. Without question, any whisper of some new ceramic technique or improvement would have excited curiosity—and if factory workmen could be bribed into releasing vital information, every effort would have been made to discover the secrets.

Dwight's 'misterie and invencon', as it was referred to in Patent No. 164 of 1671, and his monopoly must have been common knowledge amongst the potters of his day in various parts of the country; and he received additional publicity when, in 1674, he was called before a committee of the House of Lords to give evidence on the state of the pottery trade when a bill was introduced 'For Encouraging the Manufacturers of England'. Dwight's assertion that the English potters could make any sort of pottery imported from Holland except china is, to say the least, ironic when one considers that his patent for making stoneware did not lapse until 1685.

When his application for a second patent was granted in 1684, no doubt Dwight considered his monopoly inviolate for a further term of fourteen years. This, however, was not to be. It is my opinion that, even before the expiration of the initial patent, salt-glazed stoneware was made elsewhere; and I see no reason to dispute the evidence given by John Hearne during the 1693 law-suit that in about 1673 he, as well as the younger Symon Woolters, had made stoneware for Mr. Killigrew of Chelsea and also that a Mr. Sands had later hired him to make the same type of stoneware.

Ignoring the patents and risking the consequences, several potters openly began to manufacture stoneware coated with a salt-glaze. Dwight, on learning that his rights were being infringed, started to collect evidence in support of a series of actions against the offenders. These law-suits in the Court of Chancery were to drag on from 1693 to 1697.

It was claimed in the first case, lodged in the Court of Chancery on the 20th June 1693, that one of Dwight's labourers, John Chandler, had been enticed from his service by John and David Elers of Fulham (later of Bradwell, Staffordshire) and James Morley of Nottingham. On the 15th December 1693, permission was granted to attach the names of three more potters to the charge as Dwight widened his search. This trio of Wedgwoods is, for the purpose of our study, most important because the Wedgwoods carried on their trade in Burslem, Staffordshire. Some writers have suggested that the relationship of these defendants was father and sons, but I prefer to think that when the Court proceedings record the name of Aaron Wedgwood the reference is to the younger Aaron (1666–1743) and his brothers Thomas (1655–1717) and Richard (1668–1718). Elsewhere we learn that Aaron Wedgwood had his factory 'in the middle of the town' (of Burslem). Dr. Thomas Wedgwood is described a 'master-potter of the Red Lyon' and Richard Wedgwood as 'master-potter of the Overhouse'. On the 5th May 1694, the Court allowed Dwight to add yet another potter to the list, this one named Mathew Garner.

John Dwight's complaint was that the eight defendants 'did insinuate themselves into the acquaintance of the said John Chandler . . . and by promises of great rewards inticed him to instruct them . . . and also to desert the complainants service to enter into partnership with them to make and sell the said wares . . . and the said persons have actually entered into partnership together and have for several years past in a private and secret manner made and sold great quantities of earthenware in imitation but far inferior to them . . . the said counterfeits are sold at an under price . . . And the said confederates the better to colour their said unjust and injurious practices pretend that the earthenwares made by them are in no way like those invented by the complainant, but differ therefrom in form and figure and have several additions and improvements beyond those made and invented by your orator, whereas the truth is that they are made in imitation.'

Briefly, the answers to the charges of alleged infringement were as follows: the Elers admitted to making both Cologne ware and the red 'porcelain' but denied that a partnership existed with Morley; James Morley admitted to selling brown mugs; Garner stated that he had been apprenticed in about 1680 for eight years to a Thomas Harper of Southwark, potmaker, and that afterwards he had invented a way of making earthen brown pans and mugs, which he continued to manufacture. On the 19th May 1694 the Wedgwood brothers 'for delay have craved a dedimus to answer in the country' against which Dwight obtained an injunction 'until they shall directly answer to the complaint and the Court shall make other order to the contrary against them their workmen servants and agents'.

Unfortunately the outcome as it concerned the Wedgwoods is not known, their answers have not survived but there can be little doubt that situated on the fringe of the North Staffordshire moorlands some 150 miles from London the brothers continued to make salt-glazed stonewares.

In J. F. Blacker's *The A.B.C. of English Salt-Glazed Stoneware* (Stanley Paul & Co., London, 1922) mention is made of a bill of complaint in the Court of Chancery dated 4th December 1697 in which John Dwight took action against three Staffordshire potters named Hamersley, Middleton and Astbury. Blacker says nothing about the answer given by Cornelius Hamersley and I am grateful to Miss Rhoda Edwards of the Minet Library, London Borough of Lambeth for providing me with the vital reference numbers to these important documents and for the facilities given by the Public Record Office, London, which have enabled me to publish extensive extracts here for the first time.

Dwight's bill of Complaint against Hamersley, Middleton and Astbury dated 4th December 1697 (P.R.O. C6/524/37)
. . . may it please yr Lordsp that Moses Middleton of Shelton in the County of Stafford Cornelius Hamersley of Howle Ley in the Said County of Stafford and Joshua Astbury of Shelton aforesaid have entered into a confeaderacy or Partnership to make and Sell the Said manufactures or others in imitation or counterfeit thereof and with design and intent to interrupt and disturb yr Oratr in the Sole exercise & practice of the Said new Inventon and to take from him a considerable part of the inst proffitts infering thereby they the Said Moses Middleton Cornelius Hamersley and Joshua Astbury by combinaton and Confeaderacy togeather did actually enter into Such Partnership or at least did agree amongst themselves to make & Sell the Said Manufactures or Some part of them or at least to make & Sell others immitating or resembling those invented made & Sould by yr Oratr as aforesaid And the Said Moses Middleton Cornelius Hamersley and Joshua Astbury by often intrudeing themselves unknown into yr Oratr workhouses to inspect his ffurnaces and wayes of Manufacturing haveing learnt how to counterfeit the Said manufactures thereupon they the Said Confederates or Some of them by the combination and to the intent aforesaid and without any lysense or authority from yr Oratr have or hath for Severall yeares last past in a

private and Secrett manner made & Sould very great quantities of Earthen
Wares in immitation and resemblance and counterfeiting of the Said new
manufactures So invented made and Sould by yr Oratr as aforesaid and have
or hath thereby gained great proffitt and advantage to themselves and by
meanes thereof have much injured yr Oratr and prvented & interrupted him
in the Sole exercise & practice of the Said new Invention and occasioned
great loss and detriment to yr Oratr not only by depriveing of him of the
benefitt or makeing and vending great quantities of the Said new manufactures but alsoe by bringing a great disreputation upon the Said new Manufactures by him made the counterfeit made by the said Confederates in resemblance of the Said right & new manufactures made by yr Oratr being farr
inferior to them in value and service by meanes whereof people are now
become much averse to buy many of yr Oratrs Said new manufactures by
him dispersed abroad into other hands to be Sold fearing they should be of
the counterfeit sort made by the Said Confederates being by them sold at
an underprice to the new manufactures made by yr said Oratr hee ye said
Oratr cannot by reason thereof nor for severall yeares last past could sell his
Said wares for the full and true value thereof nor as he Sold the Same before
the Said Confederates invaded his just right as aforesaid and the Said Confederates doe threaten & give out in speeches that they will continue in their
Said unjust designe & all parties and Confederacy whereby yr Oratr hath
already been defeated & defrauded of a great part of the proffitt & benefitt
of the Said new invention intended by the Said Letters Patents & hindered
him in the Sale of great quantities of the Said new manufactures to his great
loss & prjudice and may and will for the time to come be further & greatly
injured & prejudised by such the ill practises and designes of the Said Confederates unless restrained by the Justice and Equity of this Honble Court
they the said Confederates manageing and transacting the Said affair with
Such privacy and Secreacy that yr Oratr cannot make Such discoverye and
proof thereof as may be sufficient to maintain any accon at Law which yr
Oratr should comense against them touching the prmises and the Said
Confederates the better to colour thier Said injust and injurious practice and
proceedings doe pretend that the Said Earthen Wares soe by them made and
sold as aforesaid are in noe sort like the said manufactures invented made
and Sold by yr Oratr nor made or contrived in immitation or by meanes
thereof but differ therefrom in form and figure and have severall additions and
improvements beyond those invented and made by yr Oratr as aforesaid and
that they themselves were the first and nue inventors of the Said nue manufactures or at least of the Same wares by them made and sold as aforesaid
wereas the truth is and Soe the said Confederates well know that the Said
wares by them made and Sold as aforesaid were and are Soe made in imitation and resemblance of the Said nue manufactures invented made and Sold
by yr Oratr as aforesaid and to gaine the reputation of being the very Same
and that the knowledge and Skill of makeing the Said wares or counterfeits
was gained or acquired by meanes or reason of yr Oratr Said or Show and
that the Said wares Soe by them made and Sold are the very same in figure

and outward appearance with those made by yr Oratr though inferior thereto in intrinsick value and service and that if there be any alteration or variance therein as to outward appearance it is onely by some addition or substraction from yr Oratrs said invention and yet notwithstanding they have hitherto practised the Said nue invention and designe and intend to continue Soe doeing contrary to all Equity and good Conscience Intender consideration whereof and for avoiding multiplicity of Suits at Law and that yr Oratr (his witnesses who could prove the premisses being all either dead or in remote places beyond seas) is altogeather remediless in the prmises by the strict rules of the Comon Laws of this Kingdom nor can yr Oratr thereby hinder or restrain the Confederates from the further use and practice of the Said invention or in imitating counterfeiting or resembling thereof but is properly releivable therein by the Equity of this Honble Court for practizing imitating or counterfitting of the Said manufacture or invention and may true and perfect answare make to all and Singular the prmises and yr Oratr be re-leived therein according to Equity and good Conscience May it please yr Lordsp to grant unto yr Oratr his Majties most gratious writt of suppena to be directed unto the Said Moses Middleton Cornelius Hamersley and Joshua Astbury thereby comanding them and every of them at a certaine day and under a certaine paine wherein to be limitted personally to be and appear before yr Lordship in this Honble Court then and there to answare all and singular the prmises upon their Corporall oathes and further to stand to and abide such further order and direction therein as to yr Lordship Shall seem most agreeable with Equity and good Conscience And yr Oratr shall ever pray &c

Answer by Cornelius Hamersley sworn at Newcastle-under-Lyme in January 1698 (P.R.O. C6/404/24)
The severall Answers of Cornelius Hamersley one of the Defends to the bill of Complaynt of John Dwight gent Complaynt
This defendt saveing & reserveing to himselfe now & att all tymes hereafter all benifitt & advantage that may be taken to the many incertaintyes insuffi-cientyes & others the imperfections of the complaynants bill of complaynt For Answere thereof or to soe much thereof as this defendt is Advised is anywise materiall for this defendt to make answere unto he answereth & saith And first this defendt Saith that he knows not what new manufactures of The complayant did invent or sett up nor dooth he take the wares made by the complaynant or his servants to be new inventions though he hath found out severall names for the same but to be parte of the potters trade & onely an impvement thereof & by the same rule that the comlaynant hath gott a monopoly for the same every person in any Arte or Styeal that is more ingenious than his fellow tradesmen than can invent a new fashion or do his work better than another though still parte of the same trade & made of the same materialls may gett a monopoly for the same which this defendant is advised is illegall & would be distructive to all Artes & Sciences and to all his Majestyes subjects who ought to have libertye to follow All whith lawfull

calling & imploys and for the support of themselves & their ffamilyes as they are capable of Soe as the same be not phibted by law nor distructive to his Majestyes Government this defendant knowes not what patent the complayant hath obteyned to any such purpose as in the bill mentioned but if any such patent there bee this defendant is informed that there is or ought to be a clause therein that the same shall be voyd If the invention there in intended to be not altogether new and reall inventions such as a monopoly may bee lawfully graunted for and therefore this defendant referrs therein to the complaynants patent when he shall thinke fitt to produce the same this defendant denyes that he hath often made any Earthen Ware with a designe to imitate the complaynants or that he makes any other ware than what prperly belongs to the potters trade but Saith that there hath been a trade of potters at Burslem in Staffordshire and at severall other townes there about where this defendant lives for the memory of man where the potters were never confined to any mode or fashion for the makeing of their Earthen ware but each potter did from tyme to tyme vary and alter the same as he thought good And as hee found best pleased his customers wherein some potters exceeded others as he believes the complaynant doth many if not most others in this kingdome but as the complaynant hath by his ingenuity found out a more ingenious way of making his Earthen ware soe this defendant hopes it is lawful for all others whose ingenuity is capable thereof to improve the same And if it soe happen that Any of those potts jugges or other earthenware made by this defendant doe avidentley prove to be some of them like the complaynants the same is noe fault nor anywise punishable though the complaynants grant were good & vallid in Lawe And this defendt denyes that hee made any of his earthen ware in imitation of the complaynants or took any patterns from them and if by accident any of them prove like the plaintiffs it is more than this defendant knowes but this defendt wnsesseth that he is seised of an estate of Inheritants where hee now lives in which there is clay fitt & useful to make earthenware with clay he thinks is better than the ordinary clay whereof earthenware is usually made and therefore this defendant beleives the earthen ware by him made is better than many other potters make and this defendant witnesseth that he doeth to the utmost of his owne skill & knowledge improve the same and make the best earthen ware hee can as hee hopes is lawfull for him to doe And denyse that he is partner with any of the rest of the defendants or houlds any Confederacy with them And witnesseth sayth without that that any other matter or thinge in the complaynants said Bill conteyned materiall or effectual for this defendant to make answere with & not herein & hereby sufficiently answered unto confessed or Avoyded traversed or denyed is true to the knowledge of this defendant All which this defendant is ready to avow maintayne & prove as this court shall award & humbly prayes to have dismissed with his reasonable costs in this behalfe wrongfully & without cause susteyned

The charges against Hamersley (Hammersley), Middleton and Astbury though specific do not give the dates when allegedly they intruded themselves into Dwight's premises in Fulham. It is, however, unlikely that the trespass occurred after 1693, because of the pending litigation; the case of the London potter prosecuting in the Court of Chancery would certainly have been common knowledge in the Potteries.

From the preceding actions, we learn that at least six Staffordshire potters were charged with manufacturing stoneware in defiance of the Dwight monopoly (some of the other names in the proceedings suggest the possibility of Staffordshire origin). At what date this ware was first made outside London it is impossible to deduce from the law-suits, where our sole guide is the cryptic statement 'for several years past'. This vague description is, however, sufficient to allow us to reach one conclusion—namely, before the Elers brothers migrated to Staffordshire, salt-glazed stoneware was already being made by indigenous potters.

A number of writers have offered a plausible explanation for the origins of Staffordshire salt-glaze by imputing independent discovery to London and the Potteries; but this claim requires corroboration from documentary sources and/or excavation. Until this information is forthcoming—and I doubt if it ever will be—all the available evidence points to John Dwight as the English innovator and the Staffordshire potters, by devious means, as the plagiarists.

In 1698, the year in which Dwight's second patent expired, evidence given before the House of Commons in support of a petition for the repeal of the 1695 tax on stoneware (amongst other goods) revealed that half of the workmen at the Fulham manufactory had been dismissed because of recession in trade. A further interesting fact emerged at the hearing when potter Nathaniel Parker admitted that prior to the duty being imposed in 1695 the demand for stoneware was greater than the supply. If this is so, one is tempted to ask why Dwight bothered to spend so much time, trouble and money on four years of pointless litigation. Whilst the Fulham potters were working at half strength, 150 miles to the north countless Staffordshire potters were preparing for a boom. The area known today as the city of Stoke-on-Trent had by the last quarter of the seventeenth century become established as the centre for lead-glazed slipware. And it was during this epoch that the foundations were firmly laid for the great salt-glazing era which was in part responsible for transforming a peasant craft into a ceramic industry.

Throughout the seventeenth century, the Tunstall Manor Court Rolls contained many references to potters—often when an indiscriminate quest for clay had resulted in a fine. For example:

1604. Pain Laid. It is ordained by the said Jury that if any person without permission who digs clay in a certain lane called Wall Lane and does not fill up the same well and sufficiently shall forfeit to the Lord of this manor for each default 6/8d.
1681. Pains are also laid on Tho. Malkin of Sneyd hamlet, potter that he fill up the pit he hath made in the lane near to the Dale Hall before 14 Oct.
1692. Fine. John Denhill (Daniel) brickman & Richard Mitchell for

III. An enamelled punch-pot and teapots, each with crabstock handle and spout. Note the punch-bowl and ladle shown on the table and the drinking glasses being used by the two men. Punch-pot, $6\frac{1}{4}$ inches high. Smaller teapot, 4 inches high. c. 1755.

digging pits in Burslem to the common injury of the people living there.

Abundant deposits of clay and coal in North Staffordshire were juxtaposed with an adequate water supply and, within a short distance, lead (used as a glaze), and iron and copper (the oxides used as colouring compounds). With all the essential raw materials to hand, and with inherent skill, the Staffordshire potters made rapid progress from the mid-seventeenth century onwards. As outside demands for the Staffordshire ware grew, more and more people were encouraged to seek employment in the Potteries. Apprentices were 'set on' to learn 'the secret, art and mystery' of the potting business as the small family 'pot-bank' expanded.

The Potteries, in the Midland County of Staffordshire, was ideally situated for supplying the major towns of England with earthenware and was better placed than any other area for manufacturing salt-glazed stoneware. At the beginning of the seventeenth century the adjoining county of Cheshire had three main salt-producing centres, in Nantwich, Northwich and Middlewich, but a short step from the 'mother-town' of Burslem. Originally, salt was obtained by the evaporation of brine, using coal for the furnaces. By the middle of the century, links had been established with Staffordshire for the supply of coal carried to the ' 'wiches' in horse-drawn wagons. Then, in about March 1670, rock-salt was discovered and mined in Cheshire.

Once the Staffordshire potters understood the techniques of glazing with salt, it was an easy matter to obtain the necessary supplies from over the border. Experimenting at first with various types of local clay and sand, the men from the Potteries were soon ready to compete with other English makers of salt-glazed stoneware. It was this competition that brought certain of their number, as we have seen, into direct conflict with Dwight in his long-drawn-out litigation.

Excavations throughout the length and breadth of the modern city of Stoke-on-Trent testify to the universal manufacture of salt-glazed stoneware. It has previously been suggested that the old 'butter-pot' town of Burslem enjoyed the monopoly, but this is not so. The six villages which comprised the Potteries all shared in the manufacture, as did many of the hamlets. Burslem, however, had a greater concentration of potters, a larger number of ovens and, consequently, a higher output than its neighbours. This preponderance during the latter part of the seventeenth century continued into and through the eighteenth century, as is shown in this extract from a case submitted by the potters to Parliament in 1762 asking for a turnpike road from Burslem to the Red Bull at Lawton, in Cheshire:

> In Burslem, and its neighbourhood, are near 150 separate Potteries, for making various kinds of Stone and Earthen Ware; which together, find constant Employment and Support for near 7000 People. The Ware of these Potteries is exported in vast Quantities from London, Bristol, Liverpool, Hull, and other Sea Ports, to our several Colonies in America and the West Indies, as well as to almost every Port in Europe. Great

c

Quantities of Flint Stones are used in making some of the Ware, which are brought by Sea from different Parts of the Coast to Liverpool and Hull; and the clay for making the White Ware, is brought from Devonshire or Cornwall, chiefly to Liverpool; the Materials from whence are brought by Water up the Rivers Mersey and Weaver, to Winsford in Cheshire; those from Hull up the Trent to Wellington and from Winsford and Wellington, the Whole are brought up by Land Carriage to Burslem. The Ware when made, is conveyed to Liverpool and Hull, in the same Manner the Materials are brought from those Places.

Many Thousand Tons of Shipping, and Seamen in proportion, which in Summer trade to the Northern Seas, are employed in Winter in carrying Materials for the Burslem ware. And as much Salt is consumed in glazing one species of it, as pays annually near 5000l (£) Duty to the Government. Add to these Considerations, the prodigious Quantities of Coals used in the Potteries; and the Loading and Freight this Manufactory constantly supplies, as well for Land Carriage, as Inland Navigation, and it will appear, that the Manufacturers, Sailors, Bargemen, Carriers, Colliers, Men employed in the Salt Works, and others, who are supported by the Pott Trade, amount to a great many thousand People: And every Shilling received for the Ware at Foreign Markets, is so much clear Gain to the Nation; as not one Foreigner is employed in, or any Materials imported from Abroad, for any Branch of it: And the Trade flourishes so much, as to have encreased Two-thirds, within the last fourteen years.

On the 16th February 1763:

A Petition of the Inhabitants of the several Towns and Villages therein after mentioned . . . was presented to the House and read; Setting forth, That the Road leading from the Red Bull in Lawton in the County of Chester, to and through Killigrew, Golden Hill, Tunstall, Burslem, Cobbridge, Hanley and Shelton, to Cliffbank, near the Town of Stoke upon Trent, in the County of Stafford, is in a ruinous Condition and in many Places founderous, narrow, and incommodious, and cannot be effectually repaired and widened by the ordinary Course appointed by Law; and alleging, that the Extremity of the said Road at each End falls into a great Turnpike Road, namely, that at the Red Bull, at Lawton, into the Turnpike Road leading towards Northwich and Winsford Ferries, where the navigation commences; and the other End, namely, Cliffbank, into a Turnpike Road leading into Uttoxeter, and so on to Willington Ferry, where the Navigation to Gainsborough and Hull commences, by which Two Navigations, the Materials for the Manufactures of Earthen Ware, carried on in that Country are chiefly brought and conveyed, and the manufactured Goods and Wares chiefly conducted and carried to their respective Markets, whereby great Profit and Advantage arise, and much greater would arise, in case the said Communication between the said Turnpike Roads was made easy and passable for Carriages; that some of the Petitioners have already subscribed, and are ready to apply immediately the Sum of Eleven hundred Pounds for and towards the Repair of the said Road, and only wait for the Power of erecting Turnpikes to reimburse them, and to complete the said Roads: And therefore praying, That Leave may be given to bring in a Bill for repairing and widening the said Road; and that the House will take the Premises into Consideration, and do therein as to them shall seem meet.

The above petition has been quoted in full to indicate the two most important routes by which earthenware was exported from Staffordshire. To the delight of the applicants, the Bill was passed. The road ultimately provided easier and more direct communication with the ports of Liverpool and Hull and was to remain the main link until 1777, when the first canal in the Potteries was opened. Some of the points enumerated in this important Bill are discussed in the following chapters; but it is worth remembering here that few informative documents such as this have survived and the original petition is, to my knowledge, the only one which specifically refers to a salt tax in connection with the manufacture of Staffordshire salt-glazed stoneware.

An official memorandum dated December 1693 contains the first proposals for new duties payable on salt. The Act, which came into force the following year, apparently met with little or no opposition. Over the years, however, attitudes changed and many petitions pleading hardship were presented to Parliament. All duties on native salt eventually ceased on the 5th January 1825: but before that, in terms of revenue to the Crown, the last decade of the seventeenth century was not propitious for the would-be manufacturer of salt-glazed stoneware. First, the duty on salt; and then, in 1695, the government decided to impose a tax on all home-produced earthenware bottles. Originally intended to remain in force for five years, the Act was extended in 1696 to all earthenware, stoneware and tobacco-pipes. Potters were required to supply the commissioners with details of kiln locations by the 20th May 1696. After firing, ovens had to be emptied in the presence of an officer; and goods unfit for sale were required to be destroyed in his sight.

Resentment of these impositions resulted in the many petitions referred to. For example, *The Commons Journal* of 23rd March 1696–7 refers to one presented by the 'poor glass-makers, tobacco-pipe makers and makers of earthen wares' against the duties on their manufactures. A committee was appointed to investigate the complaints and considered 'That the petitioners being numerous, the Committee thought fit only to hear Two or Three Witnesses to each Petition.' Those called to testify obviously made a good case, for in 1698 the duties on earthenware and stoneware were removed. Meanwhile, the tax on salt had still to be paid.

Salt-glazed stoneware was made in Staffordshire for a century, during which time countless potters endeavoured to compete for a living. Some, like the Wedgwood brothers Thomas and John, were highly successful; but the majority, who toiled with clay, coal, salt, sand and flint from the start of their

early apprenticeship often to the time of their death, remain largely anonymous. A fair proportion of their ware survives, but seldom is it possible to
link pot with potter. To find a marked specimen is the exception rather than
the rule. Parish registers, wills, deeds, trade directories and—rarer still—
account books, hiring books and crate books give the names of some of those
connected with the salt-glaze trade; but no list, however much one delves,
will ever give the full picture. Nevertheless proof of an extensive industry
may be deduced from the following table, which does not pretend to be ex-
haustive.

STAFFORDSHIRE SALT-GLAZE POTTERS

Adams, John (1652–1717) of the Brick House, Burslem
Adams, John (1716–57) of the Brick House and Hadderidge Pottery,
    Burslem
Adams, John (fl. c. 1750) Lane Delph, near Fenton Lane
Adams, Ralph (1687–1766) of the Brick House, Burslem
Adams, Richard (1739–1811) of Cobridge Gate and Bank House,
    Bagnall
Adams, William (1702–75) Holden Lane and Bagnall
Alders, Thomas, Cliff Bank, Stoke (partner of Josiah Wedgwood, 1752–4)
Astbury, John (1688–1743) Shelton
Astbury, John (c. 1750) Hot Lane, Cobridge
Astbury, Joshua, Shelton (1697 Dwight law-suit)
Astbury, Joshua (1728–80) Shelton
Astbury, Thomas (fl. c. 1730–50) Lane Delph
Baddeley, John, the elder (d. 1771) Shelton
Baddeley, Ralph (d. 1812) Shelton
Bagnall, Sampson (1720–1803) Hanley
Bagnall, Thomas (c. 1759) Shelton
Banks, William (c. 1756) Stoke
Barker, John (and his brother; c. 1750) Foley, Fenton
Beech, William (c. 1758) Shelton
Bird, Daniel (the so-called 'Flint Potter'; c. 1745) Cliff Bank, Stoke
Blackwell, John (c. 1780) Cobridge
Blackwell, Joseph (c. 1780) Cobridge
Booth, Enoch, senior (c. 1740) Tunstall
Booth, Enoch, junior (c. 1763) Tunstall
Bourne, John (c. 1772) Burslem
Bourne & Co (c. 1767) Tunstall
Brian, Samuel (c. 1765) Lane End
Broom, Thomas (c. 1760) Hanley Green
Bullock, William (c. 1758) Shelton
Chatterley, Samuel (c. 1760) Hanley
Daniel, John (c. 1720) Burslem
Daniel, Ralph (c. 1743–50) Cobridge

Daniel, Richard (c. 1765) Cobridge
Daniel, Sampson (c. 1765) Burslem
Daniel, Thomas (c. 1765) Cobridge
Edge, Samuel (c. 1710–15) Burslem
Farmer, Joseph (c. 1745–60) Lane Delph
Ford—(c. 1760) Lower Market Place, Lane End
Garner, Robert (1733–89) Lane End
Graham, John (1729–1808) Burslem
Greatbatch, William (1735–1813) Lane End
Hales, John (c. 1770) Cobridge
Hammersley, Cornelius, ? Hanley (1697 Dwight law-suit)
Harrison, John (1716–98) Cliff Bank, Stoke
Hassell, John (c. 1763) Hanley Green
Hassell, Jos. (c. 1758) Lane Delph
Harvey, Charles (c. 1755) Stoke
Heath, Thomas (c. 1750) Lane Delph
Heath, Thomas (c. 1770) Old Hall, Hanley
Hollins, Joshua (c. 1769) Far Green, Hanley
Hollins, Thomas (c. 1769) Far Green, Hanley
Johnson, Joseph (c. 1760) Lane End
Johnson, Thomas (c. 1760) Lane End
Keeling, Anthony (1738–1815) Tunstall
Lawton, Thomas (c. 1750) Lane End
Littler, William (1724–84) Brownhills and Longton Hall
Lockett, John (c. 1750) Burslem
Lockett, Timothy (c. 1750) Burslem
Lockett, William (c. 1759) Burslem
Lowe, John (c. 1758) Rotten Row, Burslem
Lowe, Thomas (c. 1758) Rotten Row, Burslem
Malkin, Jonah (fl. 1747–54) Burslem
Marsh, Moses (c. 1710–15) Burslem
Mellor, John (c. 1739) Cobridge
Meir, Richard (c. 1750) Lane Delph
Meir, Richard (c. 1750) Hot Lane, Cobridge
Meir, William (c. 1750) Fenton Low
Middleton, John (1714–1802) Shelton
Middleton, Moses, Shelton (1697 Dwight law-suit)
Miles, Thomas (c. 1685?) Shelton
Mitchell, John (c. 1730–50) Hill Top, Burslem
Palmer, Humphrey (fl. 1759–78) Hanley Green
Peat, John (c. 1752) Lane Delph
Prince, John (c. 1760) Fenton Lane, Lane Delph
Phillips, — (c. 1760) Green Dock, Longton
Phillips, John & Co. (c. 1763) Stoke
Shaw, Aaron (c. 1710) Burslem
Shaw, Moses (c. 1710) Burslem

Shaw, Ralph (1733 patent) Cobridge
Shaw, Thomas (c. 1765) Burslem
Simpson, Aaron (c. 1750) Burslem
Simpson, Carlos (c. 1750) Burslem
Simpson, Thomas (c. 1771) Hanley Green
Smith, John (c. 1766) Hanley Green
Spode, Josiah (1733–97) Stoke
Spode, Samuel (as late as 1802) Foley, Fenton
Stevens, Joshua (c. 1765) Burslem
Stevenson, Taylor (c. 1764) Burslem
Taylor, Thomas (c. 1710-15) Burslem
Taylor, Thomas (c. 1765) Shelton
Taylor, William (c. 1766) Burslem
Turner, John (1738–87) Stoke and Lane End
Twyford, Joshua (d. 1729) Shelton
Warburton, Ann (1713–98) Cobridge
Warburton, Edward (c. 1750–60) Fenton Low
Warburton, John (1720–61) Cobridge
Warburton, Joseph (1694–1752) Cobridge
Warburton, Joseph (c. 1762) Cobridge
Warburton, Thomas (d. 1798) Cobridge
Ward, Thomas (c. 1750) Burslem
Wedgwood, Aaron (1624–1700) Burslem
Wedgwood, Aaron II (1666–1743) Middle of the town, Burslem
Wedgwood, Aaron (1717–63; married Sarah Littler) Burslem
Wedgwood, Burslem (1724–62) Burslem
Wedgwood, Carlos (1726–71) The Stocks, Burslem
Wedgwood, John (1705–80) The Big House, Burslem
Wedgwood, Josiah (1730–95) Burslem and Etruria
Wedgwood, Richard (1668–1718) Overhouse, Burslem
Wedgwood, Thomas Dr. (1655–1717) 'Red Lyon', Burslem
Wedgwood, Thomas (1703–76) The Big House, Burslem
Wedgwood, Thomas (c. 1770) of The Upper House, Burslem
Whieldon, Thomas (1719–95) Fenton Low and Fenton Vivian
Whitehead, Christopher (c. 1760) Old Hall, Hanley
Wood, Aaron (1717–85) Burslem
Wood, Isa (1682–1715) 'Back of the George', Burslem
Wood, John (1746–97) Burslem and Brownhills
Wood, Josiah (1742–89) Burslem
Wood, Ralph I (1715–72) Burslem
Wood, Ralph II (1748–95) Burslem
Yates, John (c. 1750) Hanley
Yates, William (c. 1765) Burslem

Chapter II

Brown Salt-glaze

As stated in the Introduction, salt-glazing originated during the fifteenth century, in Germany, where clays capable of withstanding oven temperatures in the region of 1200°–1400° centigrade received a thin vitreous coating by the simple action of common salt being brought into contact with the oven fire. Such heat caused the salt to volatilise, and the sodium oxide which was released combined with the alumina and silica in the clay to form an impervious layer of glaze, usually identifiable by its characteristic minute pitting somewhat resembling the surface texture of orange-peel.

During the next two hundred years, vast quantities of brown salt-glazed stoneware—much of it emanating from Cologne—were shipped to England. In his *Ceramic Art of Great Britain* (Virtue & Co., London, 1878) Llewellynn Jewitt, quoting from the Lansdowne MSS. (British Museum, 108, folio 60) writes:

> In the reign of Queen Elizabeth, one William Simpson proposed to manufacture, 'in some decayed town within this realm', these ale-pots, which had till that time, been solely imported from Cologne by Garnet Tynes, by which he promised that 'manie a hundred poore men may be sett at worke'.

Nothing is known of William Simpson or of his proposed manufacture; neither is there any proof that a patent of 1626, granted to Thomas Rous and Abraham Cullin, ever resulted in the manufacture of 'stone potts, stone juggs, and stone bottells' in the British Isles.

Unless further information comes to light, John Dwight—as described in the preceding chapter—must be credited with the invention of English salt-glazed stoneware 'by methods and contrivances of his own, altogether unlike those used by the Germans'. Dr. Plot (*The Natural History of Stafford-shire*, Oxford, 1686) records that Dwight concluded an agreement with the Glass Sellers' Company in about 1677, to supply them with English stoneware bottles instead of German ones; but as we have seen from the law-suits, he was not the only potter making brown mugs and bottles in the Cologne style. In the Midland counties of Nottinghamshire and Staffordshire, stoneware was being manufactured with local iron-bearing clays during the last quarter of the seventeenth century.

A number of writers have challenged an early date for the introduction of salt-glazing into Staffordshire on the grounds that Dr. Robert Plot in his *The Natural History of Stafford-shire*, 1686, makes no mention of the technique. But it must be noted that the date of Plot's visit is unknown and could well have taken place ten years or so prior to the 1686 publication, remembering that his book was first issued in 1679. It is also just possible that the North Staffordshire potters were loathe to advertise their salt-glazing activities in defiance of the 1671 patent. As a non-potter, Plot (or his representative) could have only set down such technical information as was made available by the manufacturers. The terms used in his contemporary account support this belief. He could surely not have been expected to supply, for example, the following description of Staffordshire clays from personal knowledge:

> As for Tobacco-pipe clays they are found all over the County . . . and Charles Riggs of Newcastle makes very good pipes of three sorts of Clay, a white and a blew, which He has from between Shelton and Hanley green [Plate 1] whereof the blew clay burns the whitest. But the greatest Pottery they have in this County is carried on at Burslem near Newcastle under Lyme, where for making their severall sorts of Pots, they have as many different sorts of Clay, which they dig round about the Towne, all within half a miles distance, the best being found nearest the coale, and are distinguish't by their colours and uses as followeth.
>
> 1. Bottle clay, of a bright whitish streaked yellow colour.
> 2. Hard-fire clay of a duller whitish colour, and fuller intersperst with a dark yellow, which they use for their black wares, being mixt with the
> 3. Red blending Clay, which is of a dirty red colour.
> 4. White-clay, so called it seems though of a blewish colour, and used for making yellow-colour'd ware, because yellow is the lightest colour they make any Ware of
>
> all which they call throwing clays because they are of a closer texture, & will work on the wheel.

The black ware described above is certainly iron-glazed pottery—the so-called Cistercian ware which is recovered from almost every archaeological investigation within the 'mother-town' of Burslem.

A greater amount of documentary evidence is available appertaining to Burslem than to any other township in the Potteries. In 1765, for example, Josiah Wedgwood compiled a list of potters and the type of ware manufactured 'having examined some of the oldest men in the pottery here, near thirty years ago, who knew personally the masters in the pottery, and very nearly the value of the goods they got up, fifty years before that'. In quoting from this interesting document, the supposed value of the ware manufactured has been omitted because it is too much a matter for conjecture. Another

IV. A fine enamelled plate with moulded panels of raised seed pattern on rim. $9\frac{1}{4}$ inches in diameter. c. 1755.

point to be borne in mind when consulting this list is that the absence of the description 'stoneware' under the heading 'Kinds of Ware' need not necessarily imply that the potter in question was not salt-glazing his ware. Amongst others, Aaron Wedgwood, Thomas Mitchell and John Adams are known to have made salt-glazed stoneware though this is not apparent in the following list:

Pot-Works in Burslem about the year 1710 to 1715

POTTERS' NAMES	KINDS OF WARE	RESIDENCE
Thos. Wedgwood	Black & Motled	Churchyard
John Cartlich	Moulded	Flash
('Small') Robt. Daniel	Black & Motled	Holehouse
('Small') Thos. Malkin	Black & Motled	Hamel
Richd. Malkin	Black & Motled	Knole
Dr. Thos. Wedgwood	Brown Stone	Ruffleys
Wm. Simpson	?	Stocks
Isa Wood	?	Back of the 'George'
Thos. Taylor	Moulded	Now Mrs. Wedgwoods
Wm. Harrison	Motled	Bournes Bank
Isaac Wood	Cloudy	Top of Robins Croft
John Adams	Black & Motled	Brick House
Marsh's	Not Worked	Top of Daniels Croft
Moses Marsh	Stone ware	Middle of the Town
Robt. Adams	Motled & Black	Next on the east side
Aaron Shaw	Stone & dippt white	Next on the east side
('Conick') Saml. Cartlich	Motled	Next to the South
Aaron Wedgwood	Motled & Black	Next to the 'Red Lyon'
Thomas Taylor	Stone ware and Freckled	Next to the North
Moses Shaw	Stone ware and Freckled	Middle of the Town
Thos. Wedgwood	Moulded	Middle of the Town, now Grahams
Isaac Ball	?	S.W. end of the Town
Saml. Edge	Stone Ware	Next to the West
Thos. Lockett	Motled	Late Cartlichs
Tunstals	Not worked	Opposite
ſ('Double Rabbit') \John Simpson	?	West end of the Town
Rd. Simpson	Red Dishes, &c.	The Pump, West End
Thos. Cartwright	Butter Pots	West end of the Town
Thos. Mitchel	Not worked	Rotten Row
Moses Steel	Cloudy	Rotten Row
John Simpson, Chell	Motled & Black	Rotten Row
J. Simpson, Castle	Red dishes & pans	Rotten Row
Isaac Malkin	Motled & Black	Green Head
Rd. Wedgwood	Stone ware	Middle of the Town
John Wedgwood	Not worked	Upper House
Jno. or Joseph Warburton	?	Hot lane or Cobridge
Hugh Mare	Motled	Hot lane or Cobridge
Robt. Bucknal	Motled	Hot lane or Cobridge
Ra. Daniel	?	Hot lane or Cobridge
Bagnal	Butter Pots	Grange
Jno. Stevenson	Cloweded	Sneyd Green
? ?	Clouded	Sneyd Green
H. Beech	Butter Pots	Holdin

All of the foregoing potters worked with local clays. And despite Josiah Wedgwood's assertion that Dr. Thomas Wedgwood of the Ruffleys was the only maker of 'Brown Stone', there is ample evidence from excavations at widely separated points in Burslem that Dr. Thomas Wedgwood by no means enjoyed a monopoly. The most recent discovery of brown salt-glazed stone-ware was made during February 1970, when the City of Stoke-on-Trent Museum Archaeological Society carried out 'rescue' excavations on the site of the demolished Swan Bank Methodist Chapel in Burslem. In addition to various new types of stoneware tavern tankards (Plates 15 to 18), circa 1710, many mottled lead/manganese and black lead/iron glazed items with applied crown and 'AR' (Anna Regina, 1702–14) cypher were found in association with a few brown salt-glazed sherds bearing an impressed crown and 'AR' mark.

This site is adjacent to the George Inn, Burslem, where a cache of brown lathe-turned tavern tankards was unearthed in 1929 (*Transactions, North Staffordshire Field Club*, Vol. LXIV, page 173). Finds included several speci-mens bearing an applied pad of clay on which is impressed a portrait of Queen Anne below a crown (Plate 6) and others with 'AR' below a crown stamped into the body (Plate 9). Another example of the applied square portrait medallion below two crowns, found on an undisclosed site in Burslem, bears the legend 'ANNA DG MAG BR FRA ET HIB REG' (Plate 7) with cherub-heads at the corners. A proportion of the sherds from the George Inn are wasters (throw-outs from a potter's oven), so there can be no doubt that they were manufactured in the immediate locality in about 1710.

Not all tavern tankards carry a verification mark: some are plain, and others are decorated with simple rouletted patterns of lines or stylised floral motifs (Plates 8, 10, 11, 12). The fragmentary tankard excavated on the site of the Swan Bank Methodist Chapel, Burslem, is heavily rouletted (Plate 18). If there were any regulations attached to the use of the royal cypher, they are not readily apparent. Some writers have used the term 'capacity tankards' to describe this ware; others have called them 'measures'. But tests carried out at the City Museum, Stoke-on-Trent, do not support either of these descrip-tions as no two pots of similar dimensions contain the same amount of liquid when filled to the brim.

Numbers of mottled lead/manganese-glazed pots discovered in the same archaeological context as late seventeenth-century slipware have been found in Burslem bearing an applied or impressed 'WR' cypher. Undoubtedly, this mark continued to be used elsewhere long after the death of William III (1694–1702); but no excavation in North Staffordshire has brought to light any evidence to indicate that 'WR' marks lingered on in the Potteries. Thus, the splendid brown salt-glazed tankard, with its silver-mounted rim bearing an impressed crown and 'WR' cypher (Plate 5) must rank as the earliest known Staffordshire example, circa 1700. The lathe-turned base of this specimen is similar to the reeded base of a tankard (Plate 9) excavated at the George Inn, Burslem, and indeed very similar to the ornamental-cordoning around the base of a mug made for the Swan Tavern at Yorktown (*The 'Poor*

Potter' of Yorktown, Malcolm Watkins and Noël Hume, page 93, Figure 3, United States National Museum Bulletin, 249, Paper 54, 1967). In this Smithsonian publication it is suggested that a template was used to shape the cordoning. While this is a practical possibility which would lead to uniformity, a search through the many brown tankards at the City Museum, Stoke-on-Trent, has not yielded any identical reeding. The small cups (Plates 12 and 13) which were excavated in Burslem also display horizontal grooving towards the base, but it will be noticed that this feature varies on each of them.

During this early period of Staffordshire salt-glaze, only hollow-ware was manufactured. So far, there have been no fragments of brown stoneware bowls, plates or dishes found on any of the recorded excavations. Tankards, mugs and cups predominate, with the occasional rarity like the teapot (Plate 14) which was found on an undisclosed site in Burslem. All items under discussion were made from local clays completely or partially covered with a ferruginous wash and arguably earlier than the three tankards excavated from the Swan Bank Methodist Chapel site (Plates 15, 16 and 17), which were first dipped in white pipe-clay slip and then partially covered with an iron-oxide wash. Perhaps the most interesting discovery from this site is the brown tankard with spreading base and narrow band of rouletted decoration (Plate 18) because the overall lustrous finish is so akin to ware associated with Nottingham.

Crouch Ware

The conjecture made by W. B. Honey (*Transactions of the English Ceramic Circle*, No. 1, 1933, pages 16 and 17) concerning 'the curious name Crouch ware' being a missing class of Staffordshire product resembling Nottingham stoneware was, to say the least, an inspired guess. From 1829—when the much maligned Simeon Shaw in his *History of the Staffordshire Potteries* wrote of the Burslem manufacturers 'we find CROUCH WARE first made there in 1690 . . . the common Brick Clay, and fine Sand from Mole Cop were first used; but afterwards the Can Marl and Sand, and some persons used the dark grey clay from the coal pits and sand, for the body' and 'in the time of William and Mary, as well as Anne, very excellent Crouch Ware was made in Burslem'—controversy has persisted. Some authorities have dismissed the term as a figment of Shaw's imagination; others have claimed drab ware (see Chapter 3) as Crouch; yet others have stated that Crouch is synonymous with Crich in Derbyshire, a well-known centre for clay; and one author glibly tells us that Crouch was made for a few years only at the beginning of the eighteenth century.

Proof that the term Crouch was in common use amongst the Staffordshire potters can be found in a sales account book of Thomas and John Wedgwood, of the Big House, Burslem, which covers the period 1745–80. This important document in the City Museum, Stoke-on-Trent, provides a wealth of new information which is published here for the first time:

Sold to John Godwin, near Newgate, Bristol

			£	s	d
1763 Sep.ʳ 26	To Crate white		5.	13.	4
	To d° Crouch		1.	15.	0
Nov.ʳ 7	To Crate white		5.	9.	10
	To D° Crouch		1.	15.	0

14. 16.   8

To 3 Dz Crouch more ⎫
not charged   ⎬   3. 6
                     ⎭

Sold to John Godwin, Bristol

		£	s	d
1769 Sep.ʳ 22	To 2 Crates white	9.	13.	7
	1 Crate of Crouch	1.	9.	2.

In these accounts, the most striking detail is the price of Crouch ware in relation to white salt-glaze. That it was appreciably much cheaper can only infer that Thomas and John Wedgwood were using local clay at little or no cost. It will be seen from the above that Crouch ware sold at 1s./2d. per dozen: thus, on the 26th September and 7th November 1763, Godwin was sent thirty dozen in each crate; and on the 22nd September 1769, twenty-five dozen.

Another interesting reference in the sales account book is an exchange on 'Aug. 16th 1766—by Red China for Crouch, cousin Josia Wedgwood.'

There is also a mention in a letter written by Josiah Wedgwood to Thomas Bentley on the 14th January 1777; 'My head clerk, Swift, is commenc'd Master Potter . . . He is join'd . . . with Cobb . . . in a work of Critch ware, such as Mr. Hayward was concern'd in at Chesterfield.' This enlightening communication proves the interchange of the term Crouch with Critch; and the reference to Chesterfield can only relate to brown salt-glazed stoneware.

Crouch was therefore a cheap product made from local Staffordshire clays mixed with sand and given a ferruginous wash prior to being fired in a salt-glaze oven, from which it emerged as brown salt-glazed stoneware. Nor was its production confined to the Potteries, as can be seen from a 1780 sales notice in the Liverpool Advertiser:

> To be sold by auction at Mrs. Hooley's, The Legs of Man in Prescot on Tuesday 22nd February . . . several buildings very convenient for and now used as Mug or Earthenware Works, with two ovens, the one for burning the Crouch or Nottingham ware and the other for the mottled or Brown ware.

Saggars

Saggars are cylindrical containers for protecting ware during the process of oven-firing. Dr. Plot, in *The Natural History of Stafford-shire*, 1686, gives an account of their use in connection with lead-glaze hollow-ware as follows:

> . . . they doe not expose them to the naked fire, but put them in shragers, that is, in coarse metall'd pots made of marle [not clay] of divers formes,

according as their wares require . . . to keep them from sticking to one another . . . and to preserve them from the vehemence of the fire, which else would melt them downe or at least warp them.

It was not only lead-glazed ware that was liable to stick in a saggar during firing. To a lesser extent, this was also true of salt-glazed ware—as can be seen from the two saggars which were excavated during 1962 in Burslem (Plates 3 and 4), where brown tankards adhere to the bottoms of the saggars. A perfect example (Plate 2) unearthed at Sneyd Green, Stoke-on-Trent, shows the standard form of saggar with circular perforations in the wall and cut-out sections on the rim to facilitate easier detachment should the saggar and the ware become conjoined in the firing. Note the two fragments of pottery adhering to the saggar-rim, which were used to ensure uniform height —essential in the stacking of ware within the oven. Simeon Shaw explains the perforations:

It has long been well known, that Common Table Salt, or Muriate of Soda, is immediately decomposed on being gradually poured into a fire; and it was easily believed, and successfully proved that the result would be similar, was it to be poured into a potter's oven, at a certain stage of the process during a high excess of temperature. The Saggers were therefore adapted to the purpose, by being formed with holes in their sides to admit the vapours, and the ware so placed in them, that every part might be affected . . . and the surface of all the vessels became wholly vitrified.

The trade of saggar-making is an ancient craft which has only recently disappeared from the Potteries with the passing of the coal-fired 'bottle' ovens. At one time, the saggar-maker could be recognised in the Six Towns by the cicatrices on his hands caused by 'throwing' these 'grog'-reinforced containers made from heavy grey marl. His wages were never high, even in the twentieth century; and sometimes he was also fireman for the 'pot-bank', as Thomas Whieldon records in his account book (held by the City Museum, Stoke-on-Trent):

hireing Servants for 1751.
Jan. 11. then hired Saml Jackson for throwing Sagers & firing p week.
    8. o (eight shillings)

In Thomas and John Wedgwood's wage and hiring book (City Museum Stoke-on-Trent) are the following entries:

Hired Thos Simpson for ye year 1766 at 6/6 (per week) he is to throw John Harrisons sagers I am certain I p^d him w^n hired him above either 2/6 or 5/– his Earnest he says I paid him none However I have p^d him now 10/–. Oct: 11 1765.
1767. Oct 7. Hiered Thomas Simpson for 6s. 6d. per week 7s. 6d. Earnest he is to throw Carloss Wedgwoods shragers I have this day gave him 1s toward his Earnest of 7/6.

Factory Conditions

No contemporary accounts have survived of the conditions which existed in the Staffordshire Potteries during the reigns of William III (1694–1702), Queen Anne (1702–14) or the first two Georges (George I, 1714–27; George II, 1727–60). Brown salt-glazed stoneware continues to be excavated, but little or no new information can be gleaned about the succession of potters who made it. The large well-organised manufactory was, as yet, a dream; and the family pot-bank, with its oven set on a smallholding, was kept working for forty-six weeks out of the year. For our earliest description of Burslem and its vicinity during the salt-glaze era we have to rely again on Simeon Shaw (*History of the Staffordshire Potteries*, Hanley, 1829), who collected his information from the older inhabitants of the Potteries,

> In consequence of its situation on an elevated portion of the Moorland Ridge, it probably never experienced disadvantage, however much its inhabitants were formerly, for a few hours at a time, incommoded by the vast volumes of dense clouds of vapour proceeding from the ovens at the time of employing Salt for the purpose of causing the glazed inside and outside of the Pottery. They were always dispersed in a few hours; and never could become stagnant, because of the constant current of air from the hills of Derbyshire, or from the sea, over the Cheshire water bason.

How different is this description from Solon's rather lurid account (*The Art of the Old English Potter*, Derby, 1883):

> . . . the smoke emitted was so dense that the passer-by had to grope his way, as in the midst of the thickest London fog, amongst fumes 'not unlike the smoke of Mount-Vesuvius'. On the scaffolds that surrounded the oven, several men stood opposite the apertures of each of the flues, shovelling the salt into the fire, and every time they fed the fiery mouths the flames, driving away for a moment the murky smoke, revealed to view the men wrapped in clothes soaked with water, and their faces protected with wet sheets.

Whatever credence one places on the foregoing, there can be little doubt that early brown salt-glazed stoneware was manufactured under primitive conditions. But alongside the slipware for which Staffordshire was then already famous, the foundations were being laid for a great industry—an industry in which salt-glazing played no mean part.

Chapter III

Drab Ware

Contrary to the opinion given by several writers, 'drab ware' is not an altern-ative description for Crouch ware but is in a class by itself. Conflicting opinion as to the merits of this branch of salt-glazed stoneware ranges from 'an unpleasing drab or buff colour' to 'this beautiful manufacture'. Sir Arthur Church's appraisal comes nearest to the truth when, in *English Earthenware* (Victoria and Albert Museum. H.M.S.O., Revised edition, 1911), he states:

> The sharp archaic designs, the wafer-like thinness, and the other charac-teristics of this ware are perhaps best seen upon the richly decorated sauce-boats, tea-pots and pickle or sweetmeat trays which form the chief treasures of collectors of this beautiful pottery. There can be no doubt that these things are far more worthy of preservation than many of the English porcelains and earthenwares which command high prices at sales and form the usual objects of worship amongst the devotees of bric-a-brac. They are original, but avoid meaningless extravagances of form and decoration and hold their own in competition with most of the highly esteemed wares of European origin.

No excuses are offered for quoting Church at length. His statement re-garding Staffordshire drab ware needs to be re-echoed; for of all ceramics emanating from the Potteries, drab ware stands high from both the technical and aesthetic standpoint. There is no reason to believe that this most satis-fying class of ware was ever manufactured outside North Staffordshire, and four of the finest specimens in existence (Plates 22 and 23) are known to have been manufactured either by Aaron Wedgwood or his sons Thomas and John of the Big House, Burslem. Along with documents, letters, sales-account books, wages and hiring books, these specimens and other outstand-ing items of salt-glaze were preserved by descendants of the Wood family until they came into the possession of the City Museum, Stoke-on-Trent.

Though unquestionably later in date than the early white salt-glaze (Chapter 5), drab ware appears to have been in production for but a short period during the 1720s and 1730s.

What inspired the Staffordshire potters to experiment towards a whiter body, apart from purely commercial considerations, is not certain. It may have been an attempt to emulate porcelain, following in the steps of Dwight; or possibly, to some degree, Lambeth delft could have influenced the early endeavours. The men from the Potteries must have realised, because of the demand for the London white ware, that their brown stone and lead-glazed slipware was inevitably destined for tavern and kitchen use and that the lighter-coloured and more decorative pots would take precedence at table— amongst the more affluent, anyway. The turning point in Staffordshire ceramic production, stimulated by changes in fashion, etiquette and general living standards, took place from about 1725 to 1730; and this important period in the history of Staffordshire pottery manufacture, when outside demands dictated output, is significant in the study of drab ware.

As we have seen, the ingredients for the various types of stoneware in-cluded brick-earth, can-marl or grey coal-measures clay mixed with fine sand from Mole Cop (or Baddeley Edge). Plot's account of the presence of white firing clays (page 18) casts grave doubts on the oft repeated statement that no white clays were used in the production of Staffordshire salt-glaze prior to the imports from Devon and Dorset in about 1720. It is inconceivable that the potters of North Staffordshire, during the experimental period, would have ignored the vast range of easily obtainable clays in their immediate locality. Applied ornament on certain drab ware (Plate 22) could, without question, have been obtained from the Shelton clay pits; and equally, there is no reason to discredit Simeon Shaw when he writes, 'Mr. Thomas Heath, of Lane Delph, in 1710 made a good kind of Pottery, by mixing with his other clay a species obtained from the coal mines, which by high firing be-came a light grey.' And although Shaw's date of 1685 is no doubt premature for the claim that 'Thomas Miles of Shelton, mixed with the whitish clay found in Shelton, some of the fine sand from Baddeley Hedge [sic] and produced a rude kind of WHITE STONE WARE,' there is nothing to preclude this experiment from having taken place. Indeed, it would have been the logical approach prior to searching for larger deposits of pipe clay.

That white clays were known and worked elsewhere in England during the seventeenth century can be seen from Houghton's *Letters of Husbandry and Trade*, written in 1694: '. . . tobacco-pipe clays gotten at or nigh Pool, a post-town in Dorsetshire, and there dug in square pieces, of the bigness of about half a hundredweight each; from thence 'tis brought to London, and sold in peaceable times at about eighteen shillings a ton, but now in this time of war is worth three and twenty shillings.'

According to tradition, John Astbury of Shelton (1688–1743) first intro-duced the white clays of Devonshire into North Staffordshire in about 1720. The price of the clay, coupled with the costs of transport, would obviously have made the importations extremely expensive; and in the early days, few potters could have afforded to do more than embellish their ware with the whiter clays. Using local clays in the manner of Thomas Heath, as described

V. A choice enamelled jug and coffee-pot with typical handle terminals. Coffee-pot, 8 inches high. c. 1755.

by Simeon Shaw, the grey or drab ware would initially have been heightened with minimum use of lighter-coloured clay—as in the case of a rare dark-grey teapot (Plate 19) in the City Museum, Stoke-on-Trent, which has a handle, spout and applied tendrils made from white pipe-clay. Other applied relief ornament in a clay stained with oxide of cobalt makes this an attractive teapot.

The sparing use of white clay on drab ware in about 1725 can be seen to the best effect on tableware, where the bulk of the pot is made from Staffordshire clay (Plates 20, 21, 23, 27, 28 and 29) with crabstock handle and spout, in the case of teapots, cream-jugs and punch-pots, in contrasting white. Sometimes, a further pleasing effect was obtained by using blue-stained clay (Plate 21) or even brown clay (Plate 20) for ornamentation.

In addition to its colour, the other distinctive feature of drab ware is the applied relief decoration obtained by using metal dies. But manufacturers of drab ware were not the first in the Potteries to employ this delicate method of embellishment. The Elers brothers, who worked at Bradwell, are credited with bringing this technique to North Staffordshire. It consisted of impressing sharply cut metal dies or stamps into pads of wet clay applied to the pot, and scraping away superfluous clay from around the edges of the die. An examination of relief detail often reveals the outline of metal dies which have indented the outer surface of a vessel with too great a pressure, as witness the cream-jug in Plate 24; or small traces of white clay can sometimes be seen where a potter has failed to clean off the extrusions,

Interlacing curves, as seen on a magnificent punch-pot (Plate 27) in the City Museum, Stoke-on-Trent, pendant ornament (Plate 20), heraldic roses (Plates 23, 27 and 28) and flowers (cream-jug, Plate 24) are some of the diverse subjects to be found on this attractive stoneware. Birds, prunus, fleur-de-lys, musical instruments (Plate 23), figures, and crosses and swags are amongst other well-known decorative features. The presence of the liver bird on teapots (Plate 20) should not automatically be interpreted as an attribution to a Liverpool potter. This popular device occurs on much Staffordshire ware; and a teapot bearing it, in the possession of the Adams family (illustrated in Nicholls' *Ten Generations of a Potting Family*, Percy Lund, Humphries & Co., London, 1931, page 10) is known to have been made by John Adams (1716–57) of the Brick House, Burslem.

All the drab ware illustrated (Plates 19 to 29) was thrown on the potter's wheel and subsequently turned when the pots were in a leather-hard state. Amongst the many examples in the City Museum, Stoke-on-Trent, there is no evidence to suggest that any of the ware was press-moulded or cast. Indeed, the clays used for drab coloured stoneware were well suited for throwing.

Certainly this type of salt-glaze can, from a technical point of view, be rated high in the long list of Staffordshire ceramic achievements. Its relatively short period of manufacture ended when the white firing clays of Dorset and Devon came into general use for tableware. The introduction of ground calcined flint into the light-coloured body (Chapter 5) produced an even whiter

D

finish which was yet another reason for the discontinuance of the manufacture of the darker drab ware in favour of what is usually described as
Staffordshire salt-glaze.

Simeon Shaw, in writing of the Burslem potter John Mitchell, sums up
the change-over as follows: 'there being at this time great demand for White
Stone Ware, Salt-glaze made with Devonshire clay and flint (and produced
by several who now desisted from using clays of the neighbourhood)'.

Chapter IV

Salt-glazed Blocks

The Burslem families of Wedgwood and Wood are inseparably linked with the history and development of Staffordshire salt-glazed stoneware from the late seventeenth century onwards. Above all others, they provided a succession of master-potters who were instrumental in maintaining the Potteries as the centre of English ceramic manufacture. Inherent skill in the effective manipulation of plastic clay, coupled with the ability to adapt to new ideas and methods of production, kept the Wedgwoods and Woods ahead of their contemporaries. Intermarriage over the years with such as the Adams, the Malkin, the Littler and the Whieldon families established a potters' élite which, through its new-found relationships, achieved an interdependence that in most cases was to prove invaluable. For example, in the fundamental business of fulfilling orders for stoneware and earthenware, eighteenth-century potters' account-books illustrate this latter point well and also show the sharp rise in ceramic production during the second quarter of that century.

By the 1720s, what could be described as a peasant craft was giving way to commercial enterprise; and though the two continued for a period side by side, the growth in number and size of 'pot-banks' brought about the inevitable change not only to the Staffordshire scene but also, ultimately, to the traditional methods of ceramic production itself. Hitherto, form and style of decoration had been dictated by the potter, whose utilitarian ware obviously met the demand. But outside influences, including silver shapes, were affecting output to such a degree that new techniques had to be evolved to supply the required complicated shapes in which relief decoration was an integral part of the pot and not applied as in the case of drab ware (Chapter 3). In short, while the thrower and turner continued to work side by side, another trade title—block-cutter—was added to the potter's vocabulary. And with the advent of the block-cutter came mass production. The Wedgwoods and Woods were pioneers in the revolutionary procedure which was to radically change factory processes.

Before discussing the important role of the block-cutter, it is necessary to clarify the terminology used in connection with two distinct methods of pottery manufacture known as press-moulding and slip-casting. Press-moulding relates to the process of pressing a thin slab of wet clay on to a shaped mould (Plates 97 and 104) or into a hollow mould (Plates 103 and 140) made from metal, alabaster, pitcher (fired earthenware) or plaster. Slip-casting relates to slip (liquid clay) poured into a porous plaster-of-Paris mould (Plates 99, 127).

Solon, in his *Art of the Old English Potter* (Bemrose & Sons, London and Derby, 1883) sums up the pressing of white salt-glazed stoneware as follows:

> As the new ware was especially admired on account of its thinness and delicacy, all efforts were made to ensure these qualities; spoons, sauce-boats and small trays were manufactured as light as wafers, by means of copper or lead moulds, which acted like our goffering irons, impressing them at one blow on the outer and inner surfaces.

An iron-bound upper and lower alabaster mould for a sweetmeat tray (Plate 30), a triangular alabaster mould for a pickle tray (Plate 31) and a heart-shaped alabaster mould for a sweetmeat tray (dated 1744) are to be seen in the City Museum, Stoke-on-Trent. All were used for press-moulded ware. The upper and lower alabaster moulds (Plate 30) should be particularly noted. To press a sweetmeat tray, a thin slab of clay was placed into the lower section and, with the upper half in position, pressure was applied. Surplus clay squeezed from between the moulds was then trimmed off and the upper section gently removed. When the pressed sweetmeat tray had dried out, it was released from the mould by pushing upwards on a stud fixed to a shaped metal plate which forms the base of the lower mould.

Tradition ascribes to the potter Ralph Daniel of Cobridge the distinction of bringing back from France in about 1745 the idea of using plaster-of-Paris moulds for casting pottery. One cannot avoid observing, however, that if the master potters of North Staffordshire were using native alabaster for their press-moulds prior to this date, they may also have been familiar with the properties of native gypsum and used it for casting.

The mould-maker was dependent upon the skill and artistic ability of the block-cutter to supply the block from which he could produce a mould using plaster-of-Paris. Without question, the end-product was largely governed by the standard of the block-cutter and his manufactures.

Most writers have claimed that an original or master model was carved in alabaster prior to the making of a block from which plaster-of-Paris moulds were taken and then used in pressing or casting. The earliest dated block in the City Museum, Stoke-on-Trent, is of 1748 (Plate 42) which post-dates the introduction of plaster-of-Paris into the Potteries. No block-maker would have been likely to spend hours carving alabaster when plaster was available.

Many of the salt-glazed blocks such as those used for spouts were directly cut and shaped from a wad of clay; others were made from two conjoined pieces of thick clay (Plate 42). But blocks for tea-ware with repeating designs

(Plate 40) were made by modelling one face in clay and, when dry, taking an impression using plaster-of-Paris and then, when this was dry, pressing clay into the negative. The two matching sections were then luted together with slip prior to being fired in the salt-glaze oven.

Painstaking concentration on detail was of paramount importance in block-making, for on the quality and crispness of the carving would depend the final result. Most blocks (Plates 32 to 47) were glazed with salt, but un-glazed specimens fired in an earthenware oven are also known. The finished block was made sufficiently solid to withstand the vast amount of handling it was to receive during the preparation of negative plaster-of-Paris moulds.

Using the block as a master, plaster-of-Paris impressions were taken from one section at a time. Oval vessels required to be made in two sections, round pots in three, square forms in four (one for each side) with a further section for the base. The number of pieces comprising the mould were then tied together to form what was virtually a negative of the block, from which a positive vessel could then be formed. Every piece of the plaster-of-Paris mould was made to dovetail closely to prevent slip escaping at the junctions during the casting process.

Though the trades of block-cutter and mould-maker are interdependent, the skills involved bear no comparison—the former being a key figure in the ceramic industry. Legends centre around such men, and above all block-cutters of the eighteenth century two names stand out: Aaron Wood (1717–85) and his brother Ralph (1715–72). Before discussing these eminent potters, it is appropriate here to outline the process of casting. For this purpose, Simeon Shaw (*History of the Staffordshire Potteries*, 1829) is cited:

> Moulds were now made of all different pieces; for complete Breakfast, Dinner, Dessert, and Supper Services, and much fancy was exercised in forming the Basket-work, Shell-work, Mosaic, Barley-corn and other patterns, with great diversity of shapes agreeably to the taste of visitors, and the ingenuity of the workman. The specimens are glazed with salt; and from the accuracy of the ornaments, and the extreme lightness, of Tureens, Dishes, and Sauce Boats, they are supposed to have been cast in the moulds, by pouring in a very thin slip and letting it remain a few minutes, then pouring it out, and refilling with a thicker slip which instantly assimilates with the former, and more than doubled its thick-ness; a third, and often a fourth dose of slip was added, until the vessels had the required thickness; when the mould and its contents were placed a while before a fire, and afterwards they easily separated, and the work-man dressed off the seams where the moulds divided, and the spouts, handles, and other appendages were affixed, in the process called Handling and Trimming.

Cast ware is invariably very light in weight; and where relief decoration is present, indentations following the contours can be seen on the interior. This typical feature is particularly noticeable on sauce-boats (Plate 129). One of the disadvantages of plaster-of-Paris moulds is that they wear out quickly, causing lack of definition in surface detail (Plate 101). When this happens, the mould-maker can take other copies from the block ad infinitum. Plaster-of-Paris moulds continue to be used in the pottery industry for both pressing and casting, though the former procedure is the minor method of manufacture nowadays.

Contrary to the belief held by certain writers, a good presser can obtain intricate relief ornamentation just as sharply defined as that of the slip-caster. It is impossible to cast in non-absorbent metal or alabaster moulds—but when these were used for pressing, relief detail was even sharper (Plate 103) than in cast examples. Recognition of this can often be an aid in identifying the process by which a pot was made; and it is worth remembering that seam-marks can occur in both modes of manufacture.

One of the finest blocks in the City Museum, Stoke-on-Trent, is for a teapot (Plates 32 and 33) commemorating Admiral Vernon's famous victories at Portobello in 1739 and Fort Chagre in 1740. A teapot from this block is illustrated in the Schreiber Collection Catalogue (Victoria & Albert Museum), Vol. II, Plate 19, Number 99. Admiral Vernon and his exploits were to become favourite subjects for Staffordshire potters during the mid-eighteenth century—neither was his ship *The Burford* (Plate 82) forgotten. Little time would have been lost in marketing pots of topical interest, so it is reasonable to assume that the teapots would have been in circulation during the early 1740s.

Another important block in the same collection is a sauce-boat (Plate 39) showing, in relief, a naked boy amongst branches of stylised peonies. This well-known subject, copied from a Chinese original in Yi-hsing red stoneware, is not confined to salt-glaze; a pitcher block for a teapot bearing similar decoration, found during excavations on the site of Thomas Whieldon's first factory at Fenton Low, is now in the Wedgwood Museum, Barlaston. Sometimes referred to as the India boy pattern, it also occurs on Staffordshire redware (*English Ceramic Circle Transactions*, Vol. 4, Part 5, page 8, Plate 6a, 6b) circa 1750.

Among the fine collection of blocks in the City Museum, Stoke-on-Trent, is the important fragment excavated during 1957 on the site of the Longton Hall porcelain factory depicting a Chinese boy astride a crouching monster (Plate 38; and see Catalogue, Glaisher Collection, No. 794); a shell sweetmeat dish, teapot and cup (Plate 40); a soup dish (Plate 43); and a sauce-boat made by the unidentified block-cutter 'IS' (Plate 35). Fortunately, many of the blocks are marked with the initials 'R.W.' or 'Ralph Wood', and in some instances they are dated. For these we are indebted to Enoch Wood, for when his house in Fountain Square, Burslem, was demolished forty-seven blocks are reputed to have been found, including one for a sauce-boat (Plate 42), one for a cornucopia (Plate 34), and the upper and lower section of a peach-patterned jelly mould inscribed 'Ralph Wood 1770' (Plates 46 and 47).

Though tradition claims Ralph's brother Aaron as 'the celebrated block-cutter', few of his works survive (one for a spittoon is in the British Museum inscribed 'Aaron Wood'). Ralph Wood, on the other hand, is well represented.

With the aid of hitherto unpublished documents, it is now possible to identify the two blocks inscribed 'Ralph Wood 1768' (Plate 44) as a 'Turk's Cap' and a 'Double Star petty'—for in the Thomas and John Wedgwood account book (City Museum, Stoke-on-Trent), they sold Anthony Keeling of Tunstall in 1772: '4 Doz double Starr pettys—3/8d'. 'Turk's Caps' are frequently mentioned, as are 'Pyramids' (Plate 45). For example, on the 24th September 1770 the Wedgwood brothers sold '14 large pyramids and 11 fluted Pyramids' for 8s. 4d.

One of the most startling facts to emerge from these highly important manuscripts is the role played by the elder Ralph Wood. Far from being a successful self-employed master-potter, he appears to have been a leading block-cutter for part of his life in the employ of Thomas and John Wedgwood of the Big House, Burslem. The many blocks made by Ralph Wood which survive cover the period 1748 to 1770. Unfortunately, the earlier account and hiring books by Thomas and John Wedgwood are missing; but one hiring book in the possession of the City Museum, Stoke-on-Trent, has the following significant entry:

> Note I gave Ralph Wood 20/– tho' I hired for 9/– a week and said no Earnest this was for ye year ending 1758 I do not remember that
> he has been hired or any money for Earnest Since this 25 Jan 1763.

Ralph Wood II was also in the employ of the Wedgwood brothers for a time, as witnessed by the following entry:

> Hired young Ralph Wood for 6/6 (per week) no Earnest for the year 1769.

The hiring book—kept, apparently, by John Wedgwood—contains further references to the elder Wood, who may have acted as his manager when Wedgwood was away from the factory for twelve months at a time.

> Left off work Nov: 11 1767 but kept Ralph Wood on work.
> Began again Nov: 11 1768 & left off Nov: 11 1769 but kept Ralph Wood on work 1770.
> Ralph Wood left off work in the Spring 1772 and Died the latter end of the year & his daughter Sarah died a little before him & his son John and Ralph left off that year.

It is obvious that Wood's links with the Wedgwood brothers were close, as can be seen from the following reference in their crate-book:

> 1772 Decr. 11 being Fryday. Ralph Wood Died.

He was clearly no ordinary employee.

These surprising disclosures project new light on the Woods of Burslem and, even with incomplete documents, sufficient evidence is available to warrant an investigation of their situation. It is hoped that further research amongst the unpublished Wedgwood papers will provide answers to some of the questions that will inevitably arise. All one can conclude at the moment is that at various periods between 1758 and 1772 Ralph Wood and his sons Ralph and John were employed by the Big House Wedgwoods and therefore could not have been working their own manufactory at those times.

Profiles

A profile is a shaping device used by the thrower to standardise the interior form of thrown hollow-ware. Made in earthenware, metal, slate or salt-glazed stoneware, it is in the form of a thin slab with a hole in the middle for the operative's grip. Many of these potter's tools are inscribed. An example can be seen in Plate 48, where the inscription reads 'E. Vernon, january ye 14 1769'. Similar salt-glazed specimens have been found at Fenton Low, Stoke-on-Trent, inscribed 'CD 1762' and 'DM 1765'; and there is one marked 'Edward Till 1767'. In a limited way, the profile continues in use by those Staffordshire firms who have not permitted all craft processes to be subjugated by mechanisation. Fortunately, traditional skill is still much evident in the Potteries despite wholesale modernisation, and the trades of block-cutter and mould-maker continue to flourish. Long may it be so.

VI. A group of enamelled figures copied from porcelain prototypes. Bird on the rock, 8 inches high. c. 1755.

Chapter V

White Salt-glazed Stoneware

Reference has been made in Chapter II to rescue excavations ably carried out by members of the City of Stoke-on-Trent Museum Archaeological Society during February 1970 on the site of the demolished Swan Bank Methodist Chapel, Burslem. Finds included three fragmentary tavern tankards (Plates 15, 16 and 17) fabricated from Staffordshire clay or marl (clay containing sand and lime, chiefly used for saggars) which had been partially dipped into an iron slip following a preliminary immersion in a white pipe-clay slip. A completely new type of salt-glazed stoneware of a putty colour (not drab ware) was also recovered (Plate 51), together with a squat mug (Plate 52) which had been white-dipped over a Burslem clay body and coloured with a narrow band of iron slip below the rim. From associated finds, all of the above examples can be dated circa 1710.

Other white-dipped drinking vessels and jugs (Plates 54 to 58) have in common an off-white body made from Staffordshire clay and sand covered with a white pipe-clay engobe (or coating of liquid clay) which may have been obtained from between Hanley and Shelton (Plate 1) or, more likely, white clay imported from Dorset or Devon. Another feature associated with this class of stoneware is the overall crazing of the glaze, sometimes only discernible under a magnifying glass (Plate 63).

The natural progression for the Staffordshire potter during his search for a whiter product must have been first the utilisation of his local lighter-coloured firing clays and marls, and then the dipping of these, in the leather-hard state, into a white pipe-clay slip. The next innovation was the introduction of calcined flint into the dip to effect an even whiter finish.

Simeon Shaw credits John Astbury (1688–1743) of Shelton as the first Staffordshire potter to use flint: 'he first employed the flint (after it had been calcined and pounded in a mortar) in a mixture with water to a thick pulp, as a wash or dip, which he applied to give a coating to the vessels, some time before he introduced it along with the clay into the body of his ware'. Nicholls (*Ten Generations of a Potting Family*, Percy Lund, Humphries & Co., London, 1931) at first favours 'Joshua Heath of Shelton—the first English potter to introduce calcined flint in 1720 instead of a fine white sand'; but later in his book he supports Simeon Shaw: 'John Astbury of Shelton and his brothers Thomas and Samuel not only improved the whitening of the clay body with calcined fine, ground flints, but introduced the whiter clays of Devonshire which perfected the white stone ware salt glaze.'

An entry in the Commonplace Book of Josiah Wedgwood, dated 15th January 1765, records further information he received from 'Steel, aged 84 —Joshua Heath or Astbury of Shelton made white ware with the addition of flint the first in Shelton. And Mr. Thomas Wedgwood of Red Lyon and Richard Wedgwood of the Overhouse, Burslem, made it first there.' And again Simeon Shaw, in recording the discovery of several pots found near the Burslem Free School in 1820, writes: 'None of these exhibit any of the white dip or wash, so prevalent in 1710—this kind of ware was much in request about 1740, and Thomas and John Wedgwood manufactured great quantities long before they erected the Big House' (1751).

The above quotations could be amplified to illustrate even further the confusion which has existed concerning the introduction of white pipe clays and flint into North Staffordshire during the first quarter of the eighteenth century.

If we accept John Astbury of Shelton as the first potter to 'employ the Pipe Clay, from Biddeford' we must, of course, discount the oft-repeated story of how powdered flint came to be used as a stoneware ingredient (Astbury is supposed to have conceived the idea after watching an ostler using powdered flint to treat a disorder in his horse's eyes) and look elsewhere for its origins. The answer is not to be found in Staffordshire archives but in the notebook of John Dwight, who recorded in 1698, when giving the ingredients for a white body, 'Calcin'd beaten & sifted flints will doe instead of white sand & rather whiter but ye charge & trouble is more.'

To scientifically test some of the foregoing technical details, the British Ceramic Research Association, Stoke-on-Trent, kindly agreed to examine the fine scratch-brown tankard shown in Plate 58 and dated 1723, and some similarly white-dipped examples (Plate 54). Sections taken through the base of each pot revealed a fairly thick engobe overlying an off-white clay (or marl) body. Analysis proved that the body contained no flint but that flint was present in the engobe. These findings were common to all items submitted for opinion, and the Research Association also made comment on the crazing of the glaze due to the poor marriage between glaze and engobe.

In the past, little or no attention has been paid to the differences which exist between white salt-glazed stoneware (body comprised of white pipe-clay and calcined flint) and white-dipped salt-glazed stoneware (body made from light-coloured Staffordshire clay mixed with sand). To the naked eye, despite the pipe-clay wash, the latter is never so white, is relatively heavier and displays a minute crazing of the glaze. Contemporary documents clearly differentiate between the two and, as one might expect—bearing in mind the cost of transporting pipe-clays from the south-west of England—dipped ware was always cheaper than the white.

Where one pot-bank was manufacturing both types of ware, separate workhouses were utilised—as can be seen from an indenture in the City Museum, Stoke-on-Trent, dated 3rd October 1752, in which John Peat, potter, of Lane Delph (Plate 1) agreed to 'demise grant set and to farm let unto John Gretton & John Edge Potters All those two Workhouses then in the holding of him the said John Peate in ffenton Vivian aforesaid one whereof is called the Whiteware Workhouse His other the Dipware Workhouse—under the yearly rent of Sixteen Pounds payable on every fifth day of May & Eleventh day of November by equal portions'.

The following extract is from the sales-account book of Jonah Malkin, brother-in-law to Thomas and John Wedgwood of the Big House, Burslem:

Decb^r. ye 12: 1747. Sold to Mr. Sampson Bagnall the first oven full of Dipt white at Eight pence per Dozen

Decr. ye 15: 1747 5 Crates packed by Ditto 25 Dozen

In Each Crate £4: 3: 4

Thus, an oven full (5 × 25 Dozen) would equal 1,500 pieces.

Jonah Malkin also records his flint purchases for 1749 as follows:

flint Receivd from Mr. Benjamen Lewis

Feb^y.	5: 1749	To	24 pecks flint	
March	2	To	12	Do
do	9	To	12	Do
	24	To	12	Do
April	5	To	12	Do
	19	To	10	Do
	28	To	11	Do
May	18 1749	To	12	Do
	19	To	12	Do
June	10	To	12	Do
July	22	To	12	Do
Agust	19	To	12	Do
Sept	23	To	6	Do
Oct	13	To	12	Do
	29	To	12	Do
Nov^r.	9	To	12	Do

There are, unfortunately, no prices given; neither are we told if the flints were already ground when Jonah Malkin received them. But as will be seen, this potter had a steady supply which was no doubt brought from the east or south-east coast of England via the port of Hull. Twenty years later, Thomas and John Wedgwood were more specific: '1769 May 3. By seventy Pecks of Ground Flint.' And their records show that the cheaper white-dipped variety of ware continued to be made side by side with the more familiar white salt-glazed stoneware well into the 1760s. A cast spitting-pot (Plate 137) circa 1750, a cast dolphin-mask spill vase (Plate 138) circa 1755, and a fine cast pierced fruit basket (Plate 145) are all examples of the later mass-produced white-dipped stoneware—much more ornate than the tankard (Plate 56), jug (Plate 57), and drinking vessels (Plate 55) made by the Staffordshire potters in about 1720.

Importation to the Potteries of white pipe-clay from south-west England in about 1720 was not a signal, therefore, to abandon the long-used clay-beds of North Staffordshire. But certainly imports increased year by year as the demand for the more expensive white salt-glazed stoneware accelerated.

To recapitulate, the body of white salt-glazed stoneware was an admixture of pipe-clay and flint; but before the latter could be used, it needed to be calcined in a flint-kiln and subsequently ground to a fine powder. In Staffordshire, some corn-mills were converted to flint-mills (a finely preserved flint-mill can be seen at Cheddleton near Stoke-on-Trent), providing a vital ancillary trade to the pottery industry. But it was soon realised that flint-dust was a serious health hazard. The first registered patent for a machine designed to combat this problem was taken out by Thomas Benson in 1726. His second patent, dated 1732, is described hereunder:

> A new engine, or method for grinding of flint stones, being the chief ingredient used in making of white wares, such as pots and other vessels, a manufacture carried on in our county of Stafford, and in some other parts of this our kingdom; that the common method hitherto used in preparing the same hath been by breaking and pounding the stones dry, and afterwards sifting the powder through fine lawns, which hath proved very destructive to mankind, occasioned by the dust suckled into the body which, being of a ponderous nature, fixes so closely upon the lungs that nothing can remove it, insomuch that it is very difficult to find persons to engage in the said manufacture, to the great detriment and decay of that branch of trade, which would otherwise, from the usefulness thereof, be of great benefit and advantage to our kingdom; that—by the petitioner's invention the flint stones are sprinkled with water, so that no dust can arise, then ground as fine as sand, with two large stones made to turn upon the edges by the power of a wheel, worked either by wind, water, or horses, which is afterwards conveyed into large stone pans, made circular, wherein are placed large stone balls, which, by the power of such wheels are driven round with great velocity; that, in a short time, the flint stones so broken are reduced to an oily substance, which, by turning on a cock, empties itself into casks provided for that purpose; that by this invention all hazards and inconveniences in making the said manufacture in the common way will be effectually prevented, and in every particular tend to the manifest improvement and advantage thereof, and preserving the lives of our subjects imployed therein.

Daniel Bird, who had a pot-bank at Cliff Bank, Stoke-on-Trent, is said to be the first to have determined the ideal mixture of flint and pipe-clay for white salt-glazed stoneware, thus earning the title 'flint potter'. Shaw reminds us (*History of the Staffordshire Potteries*, Hanley, 1829): 'the pottery made of flint and Biddeford clay, tho' very white, being liable to crack, when well fired, or suddenly heated; to remedy this, some of the native clays, and the finest white grit from Mole Cop, were used, and much improved the quality of the article'. There is ample evidence among the vast number of excavated type-specimens in the City Museum, Stoke-on-Trent, to support Simeon Shaw's statement. Though at first sight many white salt-glazed sherds may appear similar, closer examination reveals a wide body variation which can never be readily apparent in a complete specimen unless disclosed by a chip or a break.

Pipe-clay was shipped from the south-west coast, round to Liverpool or Chester, down river to the Northwich and Winsford ferries, and thence by land to the Potteries. This route became a two-way traffic: clay in, pots out.

There are many hitherto unpublished references to the purchase of clay in the sales-account book compiled by Thomas and John Wedgwood of the Big House, Burslem, of which the following entries are typical:

> 1760   Bt. Ten Tun Clay with Mr. Hartel being lodged
> at Mr. Thos Antrobus's NorthWich
> have paid Carriage for all the above after 12/– p Ton
> And have p^d. to Mr. Hartall for all the Ten Tons
> 1765 May 8. To 4 Balls of Tingmouth [Teignmouth] clay
> 1766 Jan 4. by 4 Balls p^d. again

The price of clay varied over the years. For example, in 1762 the Wedgwood brothers were paying 29/– per ton plus carriage, whereas three years later:

> 1765 Sept 29. By 14 Tons pipe clay at 26/– p Ton—£18. 4. 0

on which carriage was paid at the rate of ten shillings per ton. And seven years after that:

> 1772 July 13 By a Tun of Pool [Poole, Dorset] or Blue cast clay £2

Early lead-glazed creamware was made from the same body as white salt-glazed stoneware, and it is quite usual to find the two juxtaposed in excavations. For instance, in Greenhead Street, Burslem (*City of Stoke-on-Trent Museum Archaeological Society, Report No. 2 for 1966*), some hollow-ware fragments (Plate 75) of the 1730–40 period lay below a number of later white salt-glaze sherds which were intermixed with fragments of creamware, all having a common body. Lead-glazing and salt-glazing were carried on side by side in the Staffordshire Potteries throughout the eighteenth century; and as late as the last quarter of the century, John Wood of Brownhills, near Burslem, was manufacturing a variety of white salt-glazed stoneware, as the following extracts from his sales-ledger (City Museum, Stoke-on-Trent) show:

> 28 May 1783. 24 Doz three pint Gallipots white stone   £1 16. 0
> 27th June 1783. 13 Doz White stone Twiflers   13. 0

4th Dec 1783. 4 Stool pans white stone 11 4/– 4 D° 10 3/4	7. 4
16th Dec 1784. 12 Doz White stone Twiflers	12. 0
25th May 1785. 6 stool pans white Stone 11 6/– 6 D° 10 5/–	11. 0
28th July 1785. 7 Doz white Stone Chamberpots	10. 6
23rd Nov 1785. 24 Doz white Stone Chamberpots	£1 16. 0
30th Nov 1785. 12 Doz White Stone Twiflers	12. 0
15th June 1786. 3 Doz three pint Chamberpots	4. 6
12 Stool pans 11 Inch	12. 0
12 Jan 1787. 24 Doz White Stone cups & Saucers	£1 16. 0

The latest dated example in the City Museum, Stoke-on-Trent, is a small enamelled jug (Plate 216) dated 1773—though a teapot is recorded bearing the date 1778. White salt-glazed stoneware was therefore in continuous production for upwards of sixty years, the earliest known dated specimen being the fine posset pot in the Burnap Collection (Nelson Gallery, Atkins Museum, Kansas City), which is inscribed 'Mrs. Mary Sandbach her cup anno dom 1720' (Plate 53).

The term 'sprigging' is used in the pottery trade to describe the process of applying small press-moulded clay ornaments from a pitcher or plaster-of-Paris mould and fixing them to a pot. Occasionally, during firing, the applied details lift from the surface (Plate 61) and are then said to have 'sprung'. Sprigging should not be confused with the earlier method, described in Chapter III, of impressing a metal die on to a thin wafer of clay which has been luted to the surface of the pot—in most cases of which the impressed outlines of the dies can be seen around the intricate ornament (Plate 59). Sprigged details, such as grapes and vine-leaves, always stand out from the pot in greater relief (Plate 68), and they lack the delicacy, artistry and finish of the other method of decoration. A pitcher sprig-mould found during excavations undertaken by the City of Stoke-on-Trent Museum Archaeological Society in 1969 on the site of Thomas Whieldon's post-1747 factory at Fenton Vivian, had nine small clusters of grapes cut intaglio at intervals—much simpler than having tiny individual moulds, and obviously designed to assist speedier production.

On the 14th February 1749, Thomas Whieldon revealed in his account book (City Museum, Stoke-on-Trent) that he hired Thomas Dutton for the job of 'vineing' at six shillings and sixpence per week and paid him fifteen shillings earnest (money given to seal a bargain). On the 20th February, he took on William Cope for 'handleing & vineing & cast ware' at seven shillings per week. Also mentioned in the Whieldon account book, and of interest as an indication of the wages then current, is one of the men responsible for packing and stacking the saggars in the oven—known then, and still known, as a 'placer'. Whieldon writes:

hireing Servants for 1750
1749 hired Jn°. Austin for placeing
Jan 27 white etc. p week   0. 5. 6

Thomas Dutton, William Cope and John Austin would have worked at Fenton Vivian where, in 1969, white salt-glazed sherds and salt-glazed kiln furniture were found in profusion. Quite the most spectacular amongst the white stoneware recovered was a large portion of a bottle cooler (Shape 99, Catalogue of the Hanley potters James and Charles Whitehead, published 1798) with dolphin handles and stylised flowering plants adapted from silver (Plate 121). Enoch Wood of Burslem presented a complete specimen to the Museum of Practical Geology (illustrated in the museum's Handbook, Figure 96) which can now be seen in the Victoria and Albert Museum. During the second quarter of the eighteenth century, this shape and style of decoration was made in Saint-Cloud porcelain, so it is possible that the Whieldon example, manufactured circa 1750, was influenced by the French factory.

In recent years, excavations within the City of Stoke-on-Trent have been of prime importance in adding to our knowledge of all types of salt-glaze. A representative collection from Chapel Lane, Burslem, covers the period 1710–60 (Plate 49); but an important sherd of rare type (Plate 71), bearing the Royal coat-of-arms applied in blue-stained clay and dating to about 1735, was found in Sneyd Green during 1958. Investigation of the Longton Hall porcelain site in 1955 yielded much white salt-glazed stoneware (Plate 113), but amongst the commoner mid-eighteenth-century varieties was an unusually thick, grey type unrecorded elsewhere. These and other excavations have, of course, led to a better understanding of manufacturing techniques; and they confirm the wide distribution of salt-glazing carried on in the six pottery towns throughout the eighteenth century. Many problems have been solved by the spade. Fragments of table-ware were the most prolific, predominated by moulded plates and dishes.

Little or no difficulty should now be experienced in differentiating between press-moulded and cast ware; but some pots exhibit a combination of processes. For example, bottles made in about 1735 (Plate 69) had a thrown neck fitted into the lower globular portion, which was comprised of three conjoined press-moulded sections with a base added separately. An interesting comparison may be made with two pierced fruit baskets where one has been cast and white-dipped (Plate 145) and the other press-moulded with flowers, tree and sun designs sprigged on to the inside (Plate 146)—totally different techniques of manufacture, but both made in about 1760.

Double-walled puzzle-jugs were popular for festive occasions. One in the City Museum, Stoke-on-Trent, dated 1735 (Plate 70), is decorated with a frieze of applied motifs in iron-brown below the rim. Further effective use of applied stained clay ornament can be seen on a small teapot (Plate 72), where a rose, leaf and fleur-de-lys provide a striking contrast in blue.

It is interesting to note here an important patent, dated 24th April 1733, which though concerned with a brown body refers to a wash of white pipe-clay:

Whereas Ralph Shawe [sic] of Burslem, in the County of Stafford, earthpotter, hath by his humble petition humbly represented unto in that he hath for many years been a maker and dealer in earthenware, and during the long cause of his trade hath, with great pains and expense in making tryalls, found out various sorts of minerals, earth clay, and other earthly substances, which being mined and incorporated together, make up a fine body, of which a curious ware may be made, whose outside will be of true chocolate colour, striped with white, and the inside white, much resembling the brown China ware, and glazed with salt. The great quantities of salt which must be used therein, will be an addition to the public revenue.

A unique punch-bowl (Plate 74) corresponds with the details in Shaw's original patent.

As we have seen in Chapter 1, secrets in the ceramic business were not long kept. It is therefore not surprising that several Staffordshire potters were soon making this ware. Ralph Shaw claimed sole rights and, in 1736, sued John Mitchell of Hill Top, Burslem, for infringing his patent. The case was heard at Stafford, where witnesses proved to the satisfaction of the court that John Astbury of Shelton was the inventor and that there had been prior usage of the practice. A jury gave a verdict against Ralph Shaw; and the judge, after nullifying the patent, is reputed to have said to the anxious men from the Potteries, 'Go home, potters, and make whatever kinds of pots you please.'

An extremely rare lathe-turned unhandled cup (Plate 73) in the City Museum, Stoke-on-Trent, has a brown clay body and an interior wash of white pipe-clay slip, and it is ascribed to John Astbury of Shelton (1688–1743). The outside of the cup is not 'striped with white', as the description in Shaw's patent, so it could well have been made in about 1730 by Astbury the master-potter.

The sales-account and crate-book kept by Thomas and John Wedgwood of the Big House, Burslem, covering the years 1745–80, has provided a wealth of new information in this study of Staffordshire white salt-glazed stoneware. Pots made by these brothers were safeguarded by their descendants, together with a mass of related documentary material. Thanks to an enlightened benefactor, all are now kept for posterity in the City Museum, Stoke-on-Trent.

Collectors of salt-glazed stoneware will be familiar with a feature which might best be described as notches, seen on some handles, where small pieces of clay have been removed with a sharp tool to expose two flat faces (Plate 90). Teapots and cream-jugs displaying this characteristic, together with their associated blocks, are found in the Thomas and John Wedgwood collection (Plates 79, 89, 94, 96, 98 and 110) and correspond with a description in the sales-account and crate-book, 'white natched teapots', covering the period 1740–50. Another interesting link is a block in the Victoria and Albert Museum which matches a cast cream-jug (Plate 110; in the City Museum, Stoke-on-Trent) made by the Wedgwood brothers and inscribed 'RW 1749'. The obvious conclusion is that Ralph Wood was responsible for some of the blocks used for white notched ware made by the Wedgwoods: one of the few occasions on which, with some certainty, a pot can be linked with a potter.

VII. An enamelled tea-kettle, coffee-pot and teapot with fine flower painting on a pink ground. Tea-kettle, 9 inches high. c. 1760.

In his account book, Thomas Whieldon writes that he hired William Keeling on the 16th February 1749 'for handleing' at a wage of six shillings per week. On 'June 2nd 1749. hired a boy of Ann Blour for treading ye lathe. p week 2. o' and on 'Jan 11 1750. then hired Elijah Simpson for Turning he is to have p. week 8. o'.

Lathe-treading during the eighteenth and early nineteenth century was usually reserved as an unskilled trade for boys. But it is more than likely that, today, Ann Blour's son—employed by Thomas Whieldon for two shillings per week—would be described as a child. In the nineteenth century, child labour was still rampant in the North Staffordshire potteries and was accepted by the majority as being a normal state of affairs. We have only to examine the second report of the Children's Employment Commissions, published in 1843, to sense something of the hideous situation: 'Item 41. In the Staffordshire district instances are found in which Children are employed in the potteries as early as five years of age. Several cases are recorded in which they began at six years old. Elijah Hughes, principal, Messrs. Hughes & Co's earthenware factory, Cobridge—"There are many hundreds employed of the ages of from six to eight. Between the ages of seven and eight regular employment in this trade is common, and between eight and nine it is general" There is no reason to suppose that things were any different in the eighteenth century.

The turner who, as we have seen, was receiving a weekly wage of eight shillings in 1750 could boast that his was a skilled trade. Good turners could make or mar a pot, and their adroitness is best exemplified by some of the exceedingly fine white salt-glazed tankards with spreading base (Plate 81), candlesticks (Plate 88), 'potting-pots' (Plate 83) and jugs (Plate 115).

Thomas and John Wedgwood's account and crate-books show that the term 'toy' was not merely reserved to describe figures (as suggested by some authors) but anything in the nature of miniature pots. The following extract is for the year 1771:

```
18 Sets Flowd Toys      1. 1. 0      24 Sets plain toys   8        16. 0
18 Kettles        3 }                 24 Kettles 24 Coffee pots      5. 0
18 Coffee Pots    2 }  7. 6            8 Doz Cans 9 Doz Chot. 4d.    5. 8
8 Sets Flowd Toys       9. 4         14 Sets flowd Toys             16. 4
8 Kettles         3 }                 14 Kettles 14 Coffee pots      5. 10
8 Coffee Pots     2 }  3. 4           7 Doz. Flowd.Cans & Chots.     3. 6


14 sets Flowd Toys 14   16. 4        24 Sets plain toys   8         16. 0
14 Kettles        3      3. 6        24 Kettles        18            3. 0
14 Coffee pots do 2      2. 4        24 Coffee pots    12            2. 0
7 Doz toy flowd. Cans }              14 Doz Cans                     4. 8
7 Doz do        Chts  }  7. 0        13½ Doz Chots.                  4. 2
```

[Note the abbreviation 'flowd' means flowered, i.e. floral painted.]

E

In addition to the above items made by the Wedgwood brothers, there are references to toy candles, spoons, bottles, basins, jugs, porringers, 'pewter plates', coffee-pots, teapots, cans, cups, saucers and gally-pots. Their cousin Aaron Wedgwood is mentioned many times as a maker of toys. One such reference reads:

> 4 Doz Sortable Toys Difrent Sorts 2. 8

Fortunately, some of the Thomas and John Wedgwood toys have been carefully preserved, along with the documents, and can be seen in the City Museum, Stoke-on-Trent. A selection is illustrated in Plate 84 to show the combined skills of the thrower and turner—the smallest bowl being only three-quarters of an inch high. The specimen with a handle has a faded ink inscription on the underside: 'The Groyel of ye first . . . oven . . . Nov. 24. 1743.' Though the meaning is lost, there may be a pointer in 'first oven'. Aaron Wedgwood died on the 21st April 1743. Could it be that this handled specimen was retained as a sample from the first oven of Thomas and John as joint proprietors on succeeding to their father's potworks?

The Wedgwood brothers of the Big House (now the Midland Bank), Burslem, employed both pressers and casters to produce white salt-glazed stoneware of the highest standard. Teapots (Plates 87, 89, 90, 94, 96), bowls (Plates 98 to 100), sauce-boats (Plates 129, 131), shells (Plate 107), Turk's Caps [dated 1746] (Plate 108), jugs (Plate 110), melons (Plate 134), trays (Plate 105) and graceful cups (Plate 135) were all made by the casting process. 'Square petty's' and 'flowerd spoon boats', circa 1745 (Plate 103), pickle trays and sweetmeat dishes (Plates 104 and 105), 'fishes' (Plate 132), 'suns' and 'moons' (Plate 133), and spoons (Plates 139 and 140) were all press-moulded. References to the last-named product in the Wedgwood documents are too numerous to detail: spoons of every description were made in vast quantities. To quote but one entry:

1772 Mar 2. (sold to) Mr. Palmer		
15 Doz peirced & unpeirced spoons		0. 17. 6
3 Doz pap Spoons	10[d]	2. 6
14 Doz & better	10	11. 8
14 Doz Peirced & unpeirced D[o]		16. 4
7 Doz Peirced & unpeirced short D[o]		12. 10
4 Doz Peirced & unpeirced Short D[o] & better		
17 Doz narrow mouthed musterd Spoons		11. 4
10 Doz large Tea Spoons		6. 8
2 Doz Short musterd Spoons		1. 0
13 Bell Cups		2. 0
		£4. 1. 10

And the following extract is self-explanatory:

> Sent to Mr. Brindley for his son to take
> to America in Mar 1772

1 Doz Meat Spoons & 6 Peirced
6 Doz Tea Spoons Two sises
½ Doz narrow mouthed spoons
1 Doz short musterd Spoons
Nest Starr pettys
Nest double Starr pettys
Nest double Starr Cups Nest treble do
Nest Custerd Cups
Nest Puding Nest D⁰
3 Ash Flow^r Pots & Stands
Ash Pint & Qu^t. Jug D⁰

Before leaving the Wedgwood brothers and white salt-glazed products, an interesting reference occurs in their wages and hiring book regarding the overnight firing of ovens:

1760. Hired Benjamin Burrows for the year 1761 at 5/6 & 1762 at 6/–
12^d a Night for sitting up with white oven.

A time-honoured custom in the potting business.

Casting permitted an unlimited variety of forms for table ware—teapots, in particular, being offered in all shapes and sizes. One of the most popular was in the form of a house (Plates 89, 90 and 91). There are several variations on this theme, but the rarest version (Plate 91), made in about 1745, has a bird finial and shaped handle. Flowered toy kettles (Plate 93) were made in large numbers, as we have seen, but few have survived the passing of time. The cast shell teapot (Plate 95) was another favourite shape from about 1745 onwards.

Outstanding amongst cast ware is the 'Seven Champions of Christendom' bowl in the collection of Colonial Williamsburg (Plate 102). In this can be seen the hall-mark of a leading block-cutter, without whose skill the definition of the various saints and the accompanying legends would not have been so perfect.

For his endless variety of shapes and types of decoration, the Staffordshire potter was influenced not only by the current silver shapes but also by the early manufacture of English porcelain. The famous Chelsea 'Goat and Bee' jug was copied in white salt-glazed stoneware. A fine cast example (Plate 106) can be seen in the Burnap Collection, Nelson Gallery, Atkins Museum, Kansas City.

During the second half of the eighteenth century, wall flower-holders were manufactured both by casting (Plate 156) and pressing (Plate 155), not only in white stoneware but also in lead-glazed earthenware.

Single and double tea-caddies (Plates 117, 118 and 119) of the 1750s were slabbed and press-moulded, bearing a wide range of ornamentation. Fragments of various types of caddy were found by the City of Stoke-on-Trent Museum Archaeological Society during excavations in 1969 on the site of

Thomas Whieldon's post-1747 factory at Fenton Vivian. The Wedgwood sales-account book lists prices of tea as follows:

1757 May 26. By 3 lb Green Tea at 8/– [per pound]
                    1 lb Bloom Green 10/–
1762 May 7   1 lb Green Tea 9/– 1 lb Bohea 6/–

Another popular press-moulded product was the decorative tile, such as the one in the Metropolitan Museum of Art (Plate 120) which was made in about 1750 and is reputed to have come from a fireplace in Thomas Whieldon's house, 'The Grove', Fenton Vivian.

Charles F. C. Luxmoore (*Saltglaze with the notes of a collector*. William Pollard, Exeter, 1924) quotes a letter written by M. Solon to Dr. Sidebotham on this subject:

> Whieldon's house, now included in the Round House and Depot of the North Staffordshire Railway, is situated at Fenton. When the interior of the building was transformed into workshops, about forty years ago, all decorated parts, including the chimney pieces, were removed. One of the mounted shelves was adorned with saltglaze tiles. A young assistant of mine bought or begged the lot, and sold it in small instalments to me and other small collectors. The Hanley Museum [now the City Museum, Stoke-on-Trent] has a few examples of the same subject stained in coloured glazes.

Luxmoore adds:

> Other saltglazed examples include the following subjects: 'Farm-buildings, poultry, and a well', 'a farmyard with peacock, turkey and goose', 'Landscape and bull tossing a bulldog'.

Large quantities of white salt-glazed plates and dishes have survived, and the common varieties can still be obtained at a reasonable price. Contemporary account books list table plates, breakfast, round, square, soup and 'china rail' sub-divided as plain, gadroon, feather-edge, barley-corn, basket, etc. One small consignment of dishes made by the Wedgwood brothers of the Big House, Burslem, in 1772 illustrates the size range from ten to seventeen inches, together with the retail price:

Gaddaroon Barley & Basket

6 Large dishes	17″	16	8.	0
4	D°	16	13	4. 4
6	D°	15	11	5. 6
6	D°	14	9	4. 6
6	D°	13	7	3. 6
6	D°	12	5	2. 6
6	D°	11	4	2. 0
6	D°	10	3	1. 6

All such plates and dishes were moulded. A slab of wet clay was placed over a convex plaster mould fixed to a wheel-head and, as the wheel rotated, the plate was shaped with the aid of a template. Thus, by pressure, the obverse and reverse of flat ware was achieved with the one action. This hand-operation later gave way to the jigger (mechanical plate-maker). When the clay had dried, it was an easy matter—because of water absorption and contraction—to remove a plate from its mould even when the article was decorated with raised ornament (Plate 141). After a further period of drying-out, the edges of the leather-hard pot were cleaned up (fettled) prior to being packed in a saggar (Plate 2) in readiness for the oven. Within the saggar, flat ware was separated by bobs or stilts (sometimes referred to as spurs). Usually, three of these were sufficient; but as many as twelve or sixteen stilt marks can be found on some examples (Plates 141, 214, 215).

From the second half of the seventeenth century, Staffordshire potters were manufacturing commemorative ware. Quite the most ubiquitous white salt-glazed plate of the 1750s was 'Success to the King of Prussia and his Forces' (Plate 144). The subject was not the prerogative of any one potter, as excavations in Stoke-on-Trent prove, fragments having been found on factory sites as far apart as Fenton and Burslem (Plate 1).

An additional refinement to press-moulded dishes was piercing (Plate 147), which appears to have been in vogue during the 1760s. Trellis patterns lent themselves particularly well to this treatment which, when executed in moderation, achieved a pleasing delicate effect.

Our determined pot-burier, Enoch Wood of Burslem, deposited an oval moulded dish with alternating seed and basket rim patterns (Plate 152), modelled by his father Aaron Wood in about 1760 in the foundations of the Old Market, Burslem, in 1835. This type of decoration, one of the most popular in white salt-glaze stoneware, was also manufactured in lead glazed earthenware and creamware, the moulds being utilised for all three varieties.

During 1969, the City of Stoke-on-Trent Museum Archaeological Society, engaged in excavating the site of Thomas Whieldon's post-1747 factory at Fenton Vivian, located a biscuit (once-fired) butter-tub cover surmounted by a cow. Butter-tubs were manufactured in white salt-glazed stoneware of several shapes and sizes (Plate 136), and Thomas and John Wedgwood were selling theirs in '1763. 4 Oct. by 2 Dz. Butter pots—3/–'. It was usual to provide an accompanying stand (Plate 122), also manufactured by the process of press-moulding.

One of the finest press-moulded teapots (Plate 126) in the City Museum, Stoke-on-Trent, has clear-cut overlapping leaf decoration in relief, three lion-mask feet and a distinctive rustic handle copied from a porcelain prototype. Made in about 1750, this teapot clearly exemplifies the skill of the Staffordshire potter, who understood so well the limitations of his clay and who was the unchallenged master of white salt-glazed stoneware.

Staffordshire's most celebrated potter, Josiah Wedgwood, writing of the years spent in partnership with Thomas Whieldon (1754–59) at Fenton Vivian, stated: 'White stoneware was the principal article of our manufacture'.

Chapter VI

Scratch-blue and Littler–Wedgwood blue

Scratch-blue

The decoration of white salt-glazed stoneware by the scratch-blue technique began in about 1740 and ended in about 1780. A large punch-bowl in the Greg Collection, City Art Gallery, Manchester, is inscribed 'EG 1742'; a famous mug in the Glaisher Collection, Fitzwilliam Museum, Cambridge, is inscribed 'Enoch Booth 1742'; and a harvest flask in the City Museum, Stoke-on-Trent, has 'Bengamin Mellor, 1775' scratched on one face. Between these dates, tea-caddies, mugs, plates, cups, bowls, bottles, punch-bowls, ale-tankards, puzzle-jugs, loving cups and harvest flasks were embellished with rather artless stylised flowers, foliage and, less frequently, birds. Such ware was particularly popular during the first twenty years of its production as betrothal, christening and birthday remembrances; but from the surviving numbers of puzzle-jugs and pots marked 'Ale', it is evident that they were also intended for other convivial occasions. Incised on a plain white quart-sized mug in the Victoria and Albert Museum is the name of the owner—'William Bell, 1747'. Mugs such as this were in demand as souvenirs, and the desire to have one's name indelibly engraved in clay ensured good trade for the potter.

Simeon Shaw (*History of the Staffordshire Potteries*, 1829) wrote:

> The Flowerers now scratched the jugs and tea ware, with a sharp pointed nail, and filled the interstices with ground zaffre, in rude imitation of the unmeaning scenery on foreign porcelain; and in this art women were instructed, as a constant demand was made on the men for the plastic branches.

Zaffre was the impure oxide obtained by partially roasting cobalt ore which had been previously mixed with two or three times its weight of fine sand. A purer form, called smalt (sometimes written as 'smales'), was known to the potter Christian Wilhelm of Southwark who, in 1628, petitioned the King for permission to manufacture 'blue starch, alias smalt'. Wilhelm complained that one Abraham Baker had the monopoly, and ten years later he again petitioned the King—this time to withdraw that privilege from Baker.

Long before zaffre was introduced into Staffordshire, it was mentioned in Dwight's pocket-book:

> 1691 March 15. *To make a blew porcellane Cley to be turn'd into vessells or to spot and inlay pots of any other Porcellane*—
> Take fiue pounds of Cley, fiue pound of ye fine White Earth, one pound of zaffer fine ground dryd and done through a midling hair sieve, mingle & tread. If it be wetted with the white water 'twill be the brighter.

The Staffordshire historian again mentions zaffre in relation to blue painting:

> In the early practice of Blue Painting, the Colours were prepared by merely grinding with a muller on a stone, the zaffres, and the Crystals of Cobalt first brought into this Country by Mr. Mark Walklett, and Mr. John Blackwell of Cobridge, exceeding fine in quality and readily used as above.

Note that Shaw, in this reference, draws the distinction between zaffre and cobalt crystals—that is, between the impure and pure forms.

Experiments in Stoke-on-Trent have shown that a mixture of clay and cobalt-oxide rubbed into the incisions of a pot in the unfired 'green' state achieves a similar appearance to that of eighteenth-century ware. As the surplus pigment had to be brushed off to prevent an overall blue cast, it was found that the best simulated effect was obtained by allowing the colour to lie in deep incisions. On a very damp body there was a greater degree of discoloration as the colour tended to spread. Cobalt-blue is a difficult colour to work with. To prevent contamination, the scratch-blue workshop would certainly have been segregated at an eighteenth century pot-bank.

Enoch Booth of Tunstall (Plate 1) is said to have been the first potter in Staffordshire to use a liquid glaze containing lead and flint on biscuit earthenware in about 1750. As mentioned above, a scratch-blue mug with a slightly spreading base and decorated with three grotesque birds, acorns and leaves bears his name and the date '1742'. A fine loving cup (Plate 166) in the City Museum, Stoke-on-Trent, has 'EB 1754' incised, with floral decoration and a narrow band of rouletting below the lathe-turned rim—and this example is also attributed to Enoch Booth. As will be seen in Chapter VII, Enoch Booth and his son Enoch were also makers of enamelled salt-glaze and had an established trade by contra with Thomas and John Wedgwood of the Big House, Burslem. Lack of contemporary documentation prevents a real assessment of Booth's standing in the pottery industry, but it is quite obvious from what is known that he was justly described as a master-potter.

The earliest dated specimen of scratch-blue in the City Museum, Stoke-on-Trent, is a unique two-handled loving cup (Plate 157) inscribed 'MB 1748'. Set amongst typical floral decoration is what may possibly represent the badge of the Templars or the Agnus Dei—and as with most hollow-ware examples, the turning is fine workmanship.

If a standard shape was favoured for the loving cup, the Staffordshire potters offered a variety of handles. Some pots had a rudimentary thumb-rest, in a number of which it was a prominent feature. In most examples, the handles were conjoined to the body; but cups are known where the lower terminal stands away from the body (Plate 158). Small cylindrical mugs or tankards were manufactured for the greater part of the salt-glaze period and many fragments have been recovered from excavations at various points in Stoke-on-Trent.

Cups and tea-bowls (Plate 159) with simple in-filled blue decoration were occasionally rouletted rather than incised—a pleasing variant amongst the floral patterned table ware. Rouletted sherds have been excavated on a number of sites in Burslem, some of the finds being oven wasters.

Technically speaking, scratch-blue jugs can be rated high when one studies the skill of the thrower and the turner; and it is usually with this form that the 'flowerer' excelled. Rouletting below rims is not uncommon (Plate 160), and during the 1750s some of the less ornate incised decoration exhibits greater freedom of execution (Plate 161). Very many fragments of this class of ware have been found over the years throughout the Staffordshire Potteries.

A rare pail (Plate 162) in the City Museum, Stoke-on-Trent with scalloped rim and twisted rope handle, is both delicate and charming in its simplicity. The restrained use of blue is a pleasing feature.

Skilfully thrown bottles (Plate 163) and double-walled perforated puzzle-jugs were two commodities greatly in demand throughout the eighteenth century. Standards of artistic ability vary. The obvious difference can be seen by comparing a puzzle-jug with the initials 'GW' (Plate 163) and a puzzle-jug inscribed 'JOHN FORD' (Plate 164), the latter being considerably more accomplished.

The larger, squat, cylindrical scratch-blue mugs invariably have a spreading base and a zone of incised decoration restricted to the upper part of the vessel (Plate 165). Simple strap handles are also a characteristic on the heavier types of mug.

Archaeological evidence from Burslem refutes the claim that tavern ware bearing 'GR' and crown stamps should be labelled non-Staffordshire. These tankards, jugs and mugs are blue-painted within curvilinear incised outlines, and the majority show the well defined marks of the turner on both upper and lower sections (Plate 168). Applied ovals of clay carry the initials 'GR' and a crown or 'GR' and a crowned head. Sherds were recovered in 1964 (Plate 167) from Greenhead Street, Burslem, and during 1967 (Plate 168) from Nile Street, Burslem, which, in an archaeological context, undoubtedly coincided with the earlier part of George III's reign. Both sites yielded factory wasters; and there are further excavated examples in the reserve archaeological collections at the City Museum, Stoke-on-Trent, to corroborate a Staffordshire provenance for this distinctive tavern ware.

'Bengamin Mellor 1775' proclaims the name of the original owner of a flask (Plate 169) in the possession of the City Museum, Stoke-on-Trent. This is one of the latest known dated examples of Staffordshire salt-glazed stoneware. If the smaller scratch-brown version in the British Museum, dated 1724, is accepted as the earliest known flask, then this class of ware bearing incised ornamentation was in fashion for at least half a century.

Littler–Wedgwood blue

Hitherto, it has been usual to refer to this branch of Staffordshire salt-glazed stoneware as 'Littler-blue'. Controversy has for long centred around the exact method by which this familiar dark blue colour was achieved, and various theories have circulated claiming it as a glaze, a dip or an enamel. Before examining new evidence from contemporary documents and the results of recent scientific examination, it is worth quoting what Simeon Shaw had to say on this subject (*History of the Staffordshire Potteries*, 1829):

> Mr Aaron Wedgwood of the Big House . . . brother-in-law of Mr. W. Littler . . . soon joined with him and endeavoured to effect some improvement in the salt-glaze . . . The manufacture of white stone pottery, was rapidly improving, owing to the ascertaining the proper proportions of marl for the saggars, and of flint and clay, for the pottery. And availing themselves of Mr. Astbury's method of washing or dipping, Messrs. Littler and Wedgwood first introduced a compound of very fusible materials—of certain proportions of ground zaffre with the flint and the clay that composed the body of the pottery; mixed with a determined quantity of water, and varied for the different kind of articles. Into this liquid the vessels were dipped, while in the state of clay very little dried, and absorbing the water, received a very thin coating of the materials in solution, which when dried and fired in the salt glaze oven, appeared of a fine glossy surface, free from those minute inequalities observable on all the Pottery glazed with salt only. Some excellent Specimens are ornamented by enamelling and gilding; and others having had a little manganese applied resemble the finest Lapis Lazuli.

Shaw is incorrect when he describes Aaron Wedgwood as being of the Big House, Burslem. This Aaron (brother-in-law to William Littler) came from another branch of the Wedgwood family and, as original manuscripts disclose, was in fact a cousin of Thomas and John Wedgwood of the Big House, Burslem. The confusion no doubt arises because the father of Thomas and John, who died in 1743, was also named Aaron.

William Littler and Aaron Wedgwood shared a pot-bank at Brownhills (Plate 1) prior to Littler embarking on his porcelain venture at Longton Hall. The earliest reference to the new colour is to be found in this hitherto unpublished extract from the sales-account book of Jonah Malkin (City Museum, Stoke-on-Trent), who was brother-in-law to Thomas and John Wedgwood:

Sept ye 10 1749. Japand flowred new Coller from Aaron Wedg^{wd}.

There is never any mention in the Wedgwood documents that the brothers manufactured scratch-blue or, for that matter, the Littler–Wedgwood blue. Items required for re-sale were purchased from Aaron Wedgwood as follows:

12th May 1759. To John Griffith. Gilded blue.

William Littler is nowhere referred to in this connection, and the following selection of entries taken from the Wedgwood brothers' sales-account book are self-explanatory purchases:

26 Ap. 1760. To Blue Ware-Aarons.
Cusen Aaron Wedgwood. 27 Ap. 1762. by 12 Midle Blew Teapots. Sec(onds).
22 Oct 1763. From Aa. Wedgwood. by Blew flowerd.
19 Aug 1763. From Aa. Wedgwood. by blue flowerd.
20 Aug 1763. From Aa Wedgwood. by Blew cups etc.

Elsewhere in the accounts there are references to 'Aaron's blue'.

From the above, it will be seen that the date range is 1749–63, during which time William Littler was manufacturing porcelain and Aaron Wedgwood was making the blue salt-glazed stoneware. If we credit these two potters with the invention, it is only right that in future their names be linked when describing this class of ware—bearing in mind that this type of product was no doubt also made by other Staffordshire potters.

The British Ceramic Research Association of Stoke-on-Trent kindly agreed to examine two typical sherds of Littler–Wedgwood blue in 1970 to ascertain the most likely method of manufacture. On one sherd, the blue layer was twenty-six thousandths of an inch thick. The salt-glaze layer on the plain side of one fragment was one thousandth of an inch thick, and on the other fragment four thousandths of an inch thick. The Association's comments are as follows:

The thickness of the blue layer rules out the possibility that it was produced by enamelling a pre-salt glazed article. The thickness is also inconsistent with dipping a salt-glazed article or with painting the green ware with colour and then salt glazing. The most feasible method of production would be to dip the green ware in a very fusible mixture containing cobalt, firing and salt glazing, the whole process necessitating only a single firing schedule.

From the foregoing, it would appear that Simeon Shaw has been vindicated.

The Thomas and John Wedgwood reference to 'Gilded blue' describes an elegant coffee pot (Plate 170) in the City Museum, Stoke-on-Trent, which has been thrown and turned. This fine example, made in about 1750, stands eight and a half inches high and has gilded floral decoration. A rare Littler–Wedgwood blue wall-tile (Plate 171) with moulded pecten-shell pattern was made in two flat sections, the blue being laid on a thin white-clay bat which is backed with a thicker slab made from saggar-marl.

Teapots with crabstock handle and spout (Plates 172 and 173) and vases of Chinese shape (Plate 173) are fairly common in Littler–Wedgwood blue; but teapots painted in white enamel (which necessitated an additional firing), such as the superb example with fine floral decoration (Plate 174), show the excellent marriage between potter and decorator.

Chapter VII

Enamelled and Printed Salt-glazed Stoneware

The invaluable Thomas and John Wedgwood documents (City Museum, Stoke-on-Trent) reveal that salt-glazed stoneware was exported from their manufactory in Burslem to most parts of England and also to undisclosed destinations overseas via the ports of Liverpool, Bristol and Hull between 1745 and 1780. 'China-men' in the metropolis were also kept well-supplied by the brothers throughout this period. The wealth of information gleaned from their correspondence, account and crate books can only make one regret that similar records compiled by their contemporaries have long since disappeared. Our picture of eighteenth-century Staffordshire ceramic production and export will never be complete; but at least we now know how the affairs of one pot-bank were being conducted.

Staffordshire salt-glaze was transported both by land-carriage and sea, as the following extracts from the Wedgwood papers indicate:

1755 June 25   p(er) sea
1755 Oct 23 LONDON   p(er) sea
1756 Decr 1
   2 Crates p Lichfield waggon & so to the Vine Inn within Bishop Gate & so by Wm Foster to Mr. Wm Graygoose in Royden in Essex
1756 Sep 1. Mr. William Perrin, 'Marlbro'
   To 2 Crates to be left at Peters Pump Warehouse Bristol for Toghills Wagon
1758 Mar 1 To 23 Crates by Capt. Record of Pretty Molly from Newhaven at Edward Sinners Pilot in Liverpool for Richards & Comber in Lewis, Sussex.

On the 26th September 1759, goods were consigned to the Liverpool potter William Reid by road to Winsford and thence by boat to Liverpool. But this was not the only route by which Staffordshire ware reached that port. For example, on the 29th May and 17th July 1760, fifteen crates went by land to Chester and then across the water to Liverpool. There was even direct consignment:

> 28th Jan 1768. Crate per William Morris by land to William Graham, Liverpool.

Goods for Newcastle-on-Tyne went by sea via the port of Hull, and ware for Dublin went via Chester. Re-routing was necessary when canals were established, as can be seen in the following:

> 1772 May 23
> Mr. Wm Kell, foot of the side, Newcastle upon Tine, To 5 Crates & carr(ied) p. Heath to Stone, to go by Mr. Henshaws boats down the canal and ordered them to Wm Fletcher, Warfinger, Gainsbrough and to his direction at Hull.

The term 'crate' must not be thought of as a container of standard size. It could vary from 88 lbs to 280 lbs. Ware was also dispatched in hogsheads—one of which, according to the Wedgwood documents, weighed 636 lbs.

Thomas and John Wedgwood sold large quantities of salt-glazed stoneware in London (as, no doubt, did other Staffordshire potters), and we know that they had contacts with Messrs Weatherby and Crowther of the Bow Porcelain manufactory as early as April 1748. Links between the Potteries and London in the early days of porcelain manufacture have been discussed elsewhere (*Transactions English Ceramic Circle*) Vol. 7, Pt. 2, 1969), and it is reasonable to assume that the Staffordshire potters were au fait with the new ceramic advances. Many examples of salt-glazed stoneware have Bow and Chelsea prototypes which could have been purchased by a visiting potter from the London factory itself or, had discretion been necessary, from a 'china-man' such as 'William Hewson of Church Lane, St. Martins, Strand' who, in September 1756, sold 'china' to Thomas and John Wedgwood of the Big House, Burslem.

The decorated London porcelain of the late 1740s would most surely have stimulated the Staffordshire potters to enrich their plain white salt-glazed stoneware. There was little danger of the cheaper Staffordshire product being eclipsed; by now, the ware was universally in demand and satisfying an ever-expanding market in table-ware. If it was the fashion in London to buy white ware which the potter had passed over to the painter for decoration, then colours would be applied to the eminently suitable white salt-glazed stoneware. But the desire to emulate the more expensive porcelain presented fundamental problems to the Staffordshire salt-glaze potter—his pot-bank was not equipped with a decorating-shop; but more important, he had no one skilled in the art of painting. 'Flowerers', scratching into the soft clay, infilling with zaffre, were available in plenty but the freehand painter or paintress was as yet unknown to the majority of small pot-banks in North Staffordshire, whose very existence was primarily concerned with fashioning from a lump of plastic clay a functional, saleable pot.

An enamel is an on-glaze ceramic pigment derived from metallic oxides such as copper, cobalt, manganese, iron or antimony plus a flux, and such colouring compounds were extensively used on white salt-glazed stoneware in the Staffordshire Potteries from about 1750. Enamelled ware required a second firing to 'fix' the colours to the pot at a temperature considerably lower than that achieved in the initial salt-glaze oven.

It must not be forgotten that, in addition to the huge output of white salt-glazed stoneware during the mid-eighteenth-century, lead-glazed creamware was also being manufactured in increasing quantity, and both types were enamelled. The historian Shaw wrote in 1829:

> . . . the enameller. This was first practised by some Dutchmen, in Hot Lane who, to preserve their operation secret, had their muffle in a garden at Bagnall . . . Mr. Daniel, of Cobridge, was the first native who practised enamelling. Workmen were soon employed, from Bristol, Chelsea, Worcester and Liverpool . . . For some years the branch of Enamelling was conducted by persons wholly unconnected with the manufacture of the Pottery; in some instances altogether for the manufacturers; in others on the private account of the Enamellers; but when there was a great demand for these ornamented productions, a few of the more opulent manufacturers necessarily connected this branch with the others. At first, the enamellers embellished merely the tasteful productions, figures, jugs, cornucopiae, &c., and the rich carved work on the vessels; then they painted groups of flowers, figures and birds; and at length they copied their breakfast and dessert sets, the designs of the richest oriental porcelain.

The potting families of Warburton and Daniel of Cobridge became specialists in the art of enamelling, and it is accepted that it was the Warburtons of Hot Lane who brought over Dutch painters and installed them at Bagnall. It is claimed that Ralph Daniel acquired his recipes for colour-mixing from his father's friend Warner Edwards of Shelton, who owned the Bell Bank— where the City Museum, Stoke-on-Trent, now stands. Edwards, who died in 1759, was partner to the Reverend John Middleton, who made the famous Walter de Checkley jug (Plates 184 and 185).

Thomas and John Wedgwood sent ware to the Warburtons, e.g.:

> 1762. Sep 24. To 2 Doz White let in one dish (teapots) to
> Warburtons

and

> 1765. July 30. To Cash to Mrs. Ann Warburton, £1. 8. 6

this amount most likely paid for enamelling done at her factory in Hot Lane, Cobridge.

Enoch Booth has been mentioned in relation to scratch-blue (Chapter VI), but he also had a decorating-shop at his Tunstall factory.

In the 1760s, he was supplying the Wedgwood brothers as follows:

1767 June 18 by 1 Doz. Enamel Teapots	7.	o
Sepr 2 by 22 Enam^{el} Tpots	9.	8$\frac{1}{2}$
Novr 5 by 18 Enamel Teapot and one Red Qt		
Coffee pot as Bill	9.	o$\frac{1}{2}$
NB one Teapot had one Broken spout		
1768 Ap^r 14 by 35 Enamel Teapots as p^r Bill	17.	5$\frac{1}{2}$

The above items cannot be confused with creamware, for on the same page we read:

1770 Sep 17 by 4 Doz cream cups and saucers	6.	o

Elsewhere in the account book, creamware is described as 'cream colour'. Thus, items sold to Aaron Wedgwood, viz.:

1767 May 29. by Enamell Teapots he had of Mr. E Booth		
as bill	7.	o

must obviously have been salt-glazed stoneware.

The Wedgwood brothers carried on an extensive trade with Humphrey Palmer of Hanley Green, who also appears to have employed his own enamellers. In this extract there can be no doubt that the pots referred to were salt-glaze:

1767 Sep 21. by 1 set of Enamel White Tea Toys

Another potter responsible for his own enamelling was John Graham of Burslem, as recorded in William Tunnicliffe's *Survey of the Counties of Stafford, Chester and Lancashire, 1787*:

Graham, John Jun. Manufacturer of white stone Earthen Ware, enamelled white and cream colour.

When enamelling was first practised in North Staffordshire, in about 1750, independent decorating establishments were essential to the potter in order to fulfil an increasing demand for polychrome ware. Until he was in a position to provide accommodation and employ his own artists, a specialist workshop such as the one operated by the Warburtons in Hot Lane, Cobridge, would have served his needs for on-glaze painting. As we have seen, by the later 1760s certain master-potters employed their own enamellers. Whether they were imported from porcelain manufactories or were locally trained workmen is not known, but from this time on the decorating-shop became an indispensable feature of every self-respecting pot-bank. Thus, by 1787 there was nothing unusual about the Graham advertisement, quoted above, offering for sale enamelled white (salt-glaze) and cream colour from his manufactory.

Perhaps the very fact of each firm employing its own enamellers to some extent has led to the anonymity which surrounds all decorated Staffordshire salt-glazed stoneware. It is rarely possible to identify a manufacturer, let alone an individual painter or paintress. Some writers have sought to analyse the various techniques and styles readily apparent in this class of ware, but their findings are largely conjectural. The Dutchmen of Hot Lane, Cobridge, for example, may have copied Chinese and Japanese designs or indeed have been responsible for decorating pro-Jacobite pots (Colour Plate II, Plate 175), but the proof is wanting and it just is not possible to identify the work of individuals. Until it can be proved to the contrary, one can only assume that the bulk of Staffordshire white salt-glazed stoneware was enamelled in that county.

We know that, outside the Potteries, Messrs Robinson and Rhodes of Leeds advertised themselves as enamellers of stoneware, that the enameller William Duesbury in London was buying 'in the white' from Staffordshire and that ware was exported to Holland and decorated at Delft. Maybe other decorators outside Stoke-on-Trent purchased plain white salt-glaze, but no information is available to refute the belief that not only was Staffordshire the great centre for the manufacture of stoneware but it was also the area where most of the enamelling was done.

Though the technique of applying bright enamel colours to the surface of white salt-glazed stoneware was essentially English, in many cases the influence of both European and Oriental porcelain is readily apparent. Coloured grounds in the Sèvres manner, as seen on table-ware (Colour Plate VII), or floral designs (Plates 189, 200 and 206) and figure subjects (Plates 192, 201 and 207) copying the Chinese style adequately illustrate this point. But the teapot, coffee-pot, cream-jug, cup, mug, jug, plate, bowl, sauce-boat, punch-pot and punch-bowl which constitute the bulk of enamelled ware display an endless variety of pleasing and colourful subjects, be it landscapes (Colour Plate IV; Plates 176, 190 and 202), flowers (Colour Plate V; Plates 198 and 200), birds (Colour Plate I; Plate 203), insects (Plates 199, 204 and 209) or portraits (Colour Plate II). Variety, however, was not limited to style and type of decoration. The enameller had an infinite number of shapes and sizes to decorate, from the cast ware (Plate 178) to the moulded (Plate 183), from the toy teapot (Plate 181), which stood two and a half inches high, to the massive punch-pot (Frontispiece) with a three-gallon capacity.

During the 1750s and 1760s, the most favoured handle and spout for teapots was the crabstock, which was enamelled to harmonise with the main decoration. Thus, a teapot with floral painting set against a white background (Colour Plate III) had a limited amount of colour applied to the handle and spout, whereas teapots with an overall decoration (Plates 187, 194, 196 and 197) usually had a coloured handle and spout. Seldom do we find the crab-stock being used in association with cast ware, but it is invariably found with thrown teapots which range in height from three to five inches. Contemporary account and crate books never give actual measurements but differentiate between sizes by referring to 'one-dish teapots' or 'two-dish teapots'. Nothing larger than this was made for tea during the period of enamelled salt-glaze. Those pots of larger dimensions, standing to a height of six inches and above, were intended to be used for punch or other such drinks. Two of these fine pots in the City Museum and Art Gallery, Stoke-on-Trent, depict a drinking

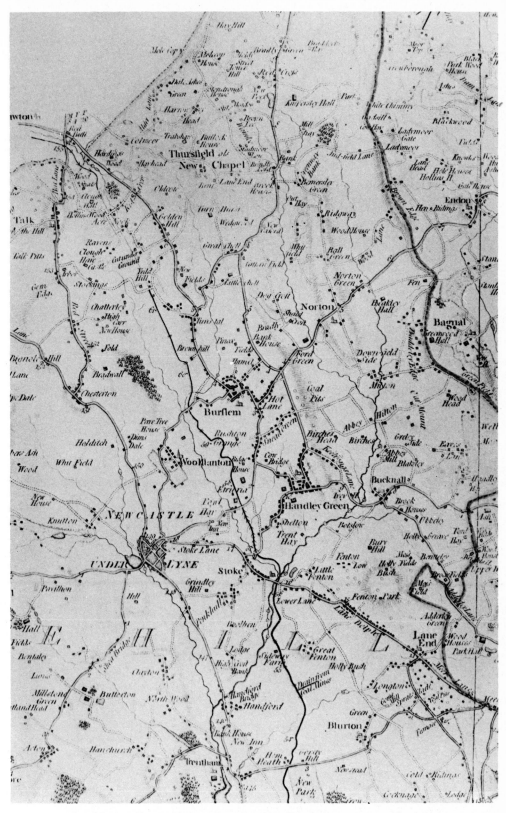

1.   Map of North Staffordshire showing the area around the Potteries. From an actual survey carried out by William Yates between 1769 and 1775.

2. The standard form of saggar (pages 23 and 47) used for salt glazed stoneware throughout the eighteenth century. The circular perforations were essential to facilitate glazing the saggar-contents during the later stages oven firing. Excavated in Sneyd Green, Stoke-on-Trent. $7\frac{3}{4}$ inches high, 13 inches diameter. First half of eighteenth century.

3. An interesting saggar, excavated in Burslem during 1962 (page 23), with a brown tavern-tankard adhering to the base. Countless saggars have been found in the Potteries but few contain complete pots. $8\frac{1}{2}$ inches high, $10\frac{3}{4}$ inches diameter. c. 1710.

4. A unique saggar, excavated in Burslem during 1962 (page 2 with the remains of four brown tavern-tankards adhering to the base. The cut-out sections on the rim facilitated easier detachmen if stacked saggars became conjoined in the oven during firi $8\frac{1}{4}$ inches high, 11 inches diameter. c. 1710.

5. A rare lathe-turned brown tankard (page 20) almost covered with a ferruginous wash and bearing an impressed crown and 'WR' cypher. The rim is mounted in silver. 6 inches high. c. 1700.

6. A lathe-turned brown tankard (page 20), with a ferruginous wash and an applied pad of clay, bearing a portrait of Queen Anne below a crown. Excavated at the George Inn, Burslem, during 1929. 5 inches high. c. 1710.

7. Fragment of a tankard (page 20), covered with a ferruginous wash and applied pads of clay, bearing a portrait of Queen Anne and the legend 'ANNA DG MAG BR FRA ET HIB REG' below two crowns. Excavated in Burslem. 3¾ inches high. c. 1710.

Below left. · 8. A brown lathe-turned tankard (page 20) with a ferruginous wash and rouletted decoration. Excavated at the George Inn, Burslem, during 1929. 8 inches high. c. 1710.

Below right. 9. A brown lathe-turned tankard (page 20) with a ferruginous wash and impressed 'AR' verification mark below a crown. Excavated at the George Inn, Burslem, during 1929. 6½ inches high. c. 1710.

10. A brown lathe-turned tankard (page 20) almost covered with a ferruginous wash and decorated with a crude rouletted and incised tulip. A crown and 'AR' verification mark is impressed to the left of the central design. 6¾ inches high. c. 1710.

11. A lathe-turned tankard (page 20) banded with a ferruginous wash below the rim and incised stylised floral motif. Note crazing of glaze. Excavated near St. John's Church, Burslem, during 1964. $3\frac{3}{4}$ inches high. c. 1710.

12. A brown lathe-turned cup (page 21) and a tavern tankard (page 20) which is decorated with a stylised floral motif. Both examples have a ferruginous wash. Excavated in Burslem during 1937 and 1927 respectively. Cup, $2\frac{1}{2}$ inches high. Tankard, $5\frac{1}{4}$ inches high. c. 1710.

13. Two brown lathe-turned cups (page 21), the one on the left excavated at the George Inn, Burslem, during 1929. The other specimen was found at an undisclosed site in Burslem. Both are covered with a ferruginous wash but the George Inn example is made from a lighter-coloured clay. $2\frac{3}{4}$ inches high. c. 1710.

14. A unique brown teapot (page 21) partially covered with a ferruginous wash. Excavated from an undisclosed site in Burslem. The short, straight spout is an early feature. $4\frac{1}{2}$ inches high. c. 1710.

Above left. 15. A fragmentary white-dipped tavern-tankard (pages 20, 21, and 35) partially covered with an exterior 'freckled' ferruginous wash. Excavated on the site of the Swan Bank Methodist Chapel, Burslem, during February 1970. $5\frac{1}{8}$ inches high. c. 1710. *Above right.* 16. A fragmentary white-dipped tavern-tankard (pages 20, 21 and 35) partially covered with an exterior 'freckled' ferruginous wash. Excavated on the site of the Swan Bank Methodist Chapel, Burslem, during February 1970. $5\frac{1}{4}$ inches high. c. 1710.

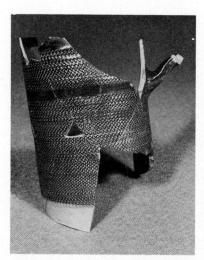

Below left. 17. A fragmentary tavern-tankard (pages 20, 21 and 35) almost covered with rouletted decoration. The lower exterior portion has been white-dipped and the remainder has received a ferruginous wash on a grey body. Excavated on the site of the Swan Bank Methodist Chapel, Burslem, during February 1970. $5\frac{3}{4}$ inches high. c. 1710.

Below right. 18. A brown fragmentary tankard (pages 20–21) covered with a ferruginous wash and a band of rouletted decoration below the rim. The lustrous finish is very similar to that of ware usually associated with Nottingham, but this example was excavated in association with wasters (oven rejects) on the site of the Swan Bank Methodist Chapel, Burslem, during February 1970. $6\frac{1}{2}$ inches high, 4 inches base diameter. c. 1710.

19. A rare dark-grey teapot and cover (page 27) with white pipe-clay handle, spout and applied decoration. The other relief ornament is made from blue-stained clay and there are traces of size-gilding. $3\frac{1}{2}$ inches high. c. 1725.

20. Two small drab-ware teapots (page 27) with white pipe-clay crabstock handle and spout. White applied ornament on the left (note liver bird) and brown applied pendant ornament on the right. Teapot on left $2\frac{3}{4}$ inches high. c. 1725.

21. A drab-ware bowl and two cream jugs (page 27) with applied ornament in white pipe-clay and blue-stained clay. Jug handles and tripod feet are in white clay. Bowl, $3\frac{1}{4}$ inches high. c. 1725.

22. A fine drab-ware milk jug (pages 25, 26 and 27) with applied ornament in lighter-coloured clay taken from metal dies and a wash of pipe-clay slip on the inside. Made by Aaron Wedgwood or his sons Thomas and John of the Big House, Burslem. $7\frac{1}{4}$ inches high. c. 1730.

23. Three drab-ware cream jugs (pages 25 and 27) with applied ornament, handles and spouts in white pipe-clay and a wash of white slip on the inside. Made by Aaron Wedgwood or his sons Thomas and John of the Big House, Burslem. Jug on the left, $5\frac{1}{2}$ inches high. c. 1730.

24. A drab-ware cream jug and tankard (page 27) with applied ornament in white pipe-clay taken from metal dies and a wash of white slip on the inside. The outline of the dies can be seen quite clearly on the cream jug. Tankard, $5\frac{1}{4}$ inches high. c. 1730.

25. A rare drab-ware vase and spill-holder (page 27) with applied ornament in white pipe-clay taken from metal dies. Vase, 6 inches high. c. 1730.

26. A drab-ware flower pot and stand (page 27) with applied ornament in white pipe-clay taken from metal dies. Flower pot, $4\frac{1}{4}$ inches high. Stand, $5\frac{1}{2}$ inches diameter. c. 1730.

27. A magnificent drab-ware punch-pot and cover (page 27) with white pipe-clay crabstock handle, spout and twig finial. Intricate applied pipe-clay ornament taken from metal dies. $7\frac{1}{2}$ inches high. c. 1730.

28. A drab-ware mug and a teapot and cover (page 27) with applied ornament in white pipe-clay taken from metal dies. The interior of the mug has a wash of pipe-clay slip. Mug, $5\frac{1}{4}$ inches high. Teapot, $4\frac{3}{4}$ inches high. c. 1730.

29. A straight-sided drab-ware teapot and cover and a depressed globular-shaped teapot and cover (page 27) with white pipe-clay crabstock handle and spout. Applied pipe-clay ornament taken from metal dies. $5\frac{1}{2}$ inches high. c. 1730.

30.　An iron-bound upper and lower alabaster mould for a sweetmeat tray (page 30). The example on the left measures $7\frac{3}{4}$ inches by $5\frac{3}{8}$ inches. c. 1740.

31.　A triangular alabaster mould for a pickle tray and a heart-shaped alabaster mould for a sweetmeat tray. The latter, dated 1744, is 7 inches long (page 30).

32.　An important block for a teapot (pages 31 and 32) commemorating Admiral Vernon's famous victories, bearing the legend 'Porto Bello taken' on one side and 'Fort Chagre by AD. VERNON' on the other. $4\frac{3}{4}$ inches high. c. 1740.

33.　Reverse side of the 'Admiral Vernon' teapot block (pages 31 and 32).

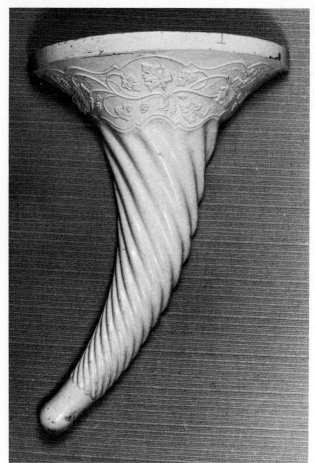

34. A block for a cornucopia flower-bracket, fluted from the base with vine leaves, and grapes above in relief (pages 31 and 32). Formerly in the Enoch Wood collection. 11 inches high. c. 1745.

35. A block for a sauce-boat marked ‡S, a leaf-shaped dish and a teapot (pages 31 and 32). Sauce-boat and teapot, $3\frac{1}{4}$ inches high. c. 1745.

36. A rare block for an octagonal teapot (page 31) with grotesque animal and bird figures in relief within oval compartments. These subjects are also known in lead-glazed earthenware. $4\frac{3}{4}$ inches high. c. 1745.

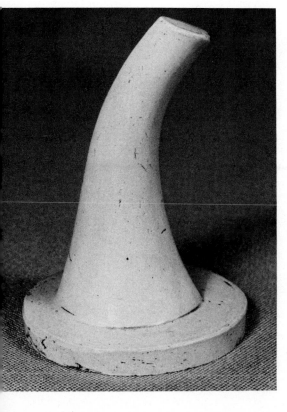

37. A block for a teapot-spout (page 31). $4\frac{3}{4}$ inches high. c. 1750.

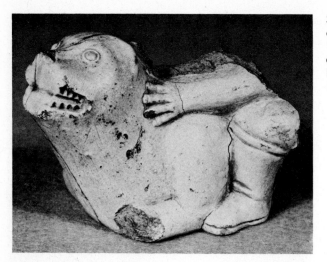

38. A fragment of a block excavated at Longton Hall in 1957 (pages 31 and 63). The complete version has a Chinese boy astride a crouching monster 3 inches high. c. 1750.

39. An important block for a sauce-boat (pages 31 and 32), showing in relief a naked boy amongst branches of stylised peonies. Subject copied from a Chinese original in Yi-hsing red stoneware. 3 inches high, $7\frac{1}{4}$ inches long. c. 1750.

40. A block for a shell sweetmeat dish, a teapot and a cup (pages 31 and 32). Teapot, $4\frac{1}{4}$ inches high. c. 1750.

41. Two blocks for sauce-boats (page 31) with beaded edge and foot. The specimen on the right, $3\frac{1}{2}$ inches high. c. 1750.

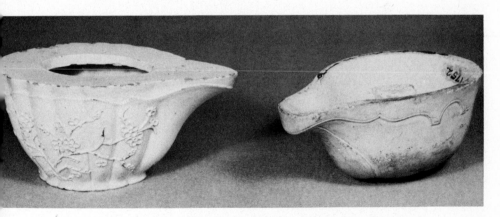

42. Two blocks for sauce-boats (pages 30, 31 and 32). The one on the left incised 'RW 1756' and the one on the right incised 'RW 1748/9'. Made by Ralph Wood I of Burslem. Block on left, $3\frac{1}{4}$ inches high.

43. A block for a soup-dish (pages 31 and 32) with floral border in relief. 10½ inches in diameter. c. 1750.

44. A 'Turk's Cap' block incised 'RW 1768' and a double star petty block incised 'Ralph Wood 1768' (pages 31 and 33). Made for Thomas and John Wedgwood of the Big House, Burslem. 'Turk's Cap,' 2¾ inches high. Double star petty, 2 inches high.

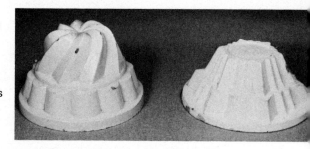

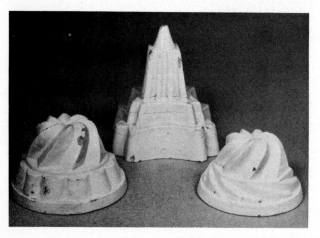

45. A pair of blocks for small 'Turk's Cap' jelly moulds and a pyramid block, all incised 'RW' or 'Ralph Wood 1770' (pages 3 and 33). Made for Thomas and John Wedgwood of the Big House, Burslem. Pyramid, 4¼ inches high. 'Turk's Cap' on left, 2¼ inches high.

46. The interior detail of an important documentary block for a jelly mould inscribed '1770 Ralph Wood' (pages 31 and 32). Made for Thomas and John Wedgwood of the Big House, Burslem. Formerly in the Enoch Wood Collection. Inscribed section, 9 inches by 7 inches.

47. An important documentary conjoined block (see Plate 46) dated 1770 (pages 31 and 32).

48. A 'profile' for hollow-ware (page 34) inscribed 'E Vernon, january ye 14 1769'. Similar examples have been found at Fenton Low inscribed 'CD 1762 and 'PM 1765'. $4\frac{1}{2}$ inches by $3\frac{1}{2}$ inches.

49. A selection of miscellaneous fragments from crouch to scratch-blue excavated in Chapel Lane, Burslem, during 1955. Note the plate sherd showing a portion of the well-known legend 'Success to the King of Prussia' (page 41). c. 1710-60.

50. A collection of miscellaneous types of kiln-furniture including bobs and stilts. Excavated in Burslem. Mid eighteenth century.

51. A unique tavern-tankard (page 35) which has been turned and rouletted. The putty colour is unusual and the glaze is heavily crazed. Excavated on the site of the Swan Bank Methodist Chapel, Burslem, during February 1970. $5\frac{1}{4}$ inches high, $3\frac{1}{4}$ inches in diameter. c. 1710.
Right. 52. A squat white-dipped mug (page 35) with a band of iron slip below rim. Excavated on the site of the Swan Bank Methodist Chapel, Burslem, during February 1970, $4\frac{1}{2}$ inches high, $3\frac{3}{4}$ inches in diameter. c. 1710.

53. The earliest known dated example of Staffordshire white salt-glazed stoneware (page 40). This fine posset-pot is inscribed 'Mrs. Mary Sandbach her cup anno dom 1720'. 6 inches high *Nelson Gallery, Atkins Museum (gift of Mr. and Mrs Frank P. Burnap), Kansas City, Missouri.*

54. A white-dipped jug and two mugs with a band of iron slip around the rim (page 35 and 36). Analysis has proved these pots to have a flint-free body and a white engobe containing flint. All three exhibit crazing of the glaze. Jug, $3\frac{3}{4}$ inches high. c. 1720.

55. A selection of white-dipped drinking vessels (pages 35 and 38), with iron slip around the rim, which have been excavated in Stoke-on-Trent. The mug on the right was found during 1969 at Fenton Vivian when the Thomas Whieldon factory site was being investigated. This mug is 4 inches high and $2\frac{1}{4}$ inches in diameter. c. 1720.

56. A white-dipped tankard (pages 35 and 38) with a band of iron slip below the rim. Found during 1968 behind an interior lath-and-plaster wall in Harracles Hall near Stoke-on-Trent. 5 inches high. c. 1720.

57. An unusual white-dipped jug with a band of iron slip on rim and handle (pages 35, 38 and 60). There is a pronounced crazing of the glaze. The size-gilded painting of two dogs barking at a cow, touched with green and brick-red, was probably added at a later date. $7\frac{1}{4}$ inches high. c. 1720.

58. A unique example—and certainly one of the earliest dated examples of a white-dipped scratch-brown tankard (pages 35, 36 and 65) with a band of iron slip below the rim. Analysis has proved the body to be flint-free, but the engobe contains flint. The glaze is crazed. $5\frac{1}{4}$ inches high. 1723.

59. A small grey-white lathe-turned mug with applied curvilinear decoration. In this example the impressed outlines of the dies are obvious—proving how such relief ornament was achieved (page 40). $2\frac{1}{2}$ inches high. c. 1725.

60. Two rare press-moulded perfume flasks heightened with iron slip. Each has a threaded hole but both stoppers are missing. The example on the left has a slabbed compartment between the heart-shaped perforations. The flask on the right was found at Caverswall Castle, near Stoke-on-Trent, during 1953 and measures $1\frac{7}{8}$ inches by $1\frac{1}{2}$ inches by $\frac{5}{8}$ inches. c. 1725.

61. A teapot and cover with crabstock handle, spout and lid-finial (page 40) with applied moulded decoration of vine-tendril, squirrel and flying insect. Note how the motif adjacent to the spout has sprung from the body. $4\frac{1}{4}$ inches high. c. 1730.

62. Three varieties of bottle, each with applied ornament. On the left, a liver bird; in the centre, grapes and vine leaves; floral motifs on the right. Centre bottle, 9 inches high. c. 1720–30.

63. A technically interesting tureen and cover (page 35) with two applied white pipe-clay handle masks and a pipe-clay handle on cover. The tureen has been press-moulded in two conjoined sections and white-dipped prior to firing. The base has been added from a separate mould and, overall, there is raised ornament of shells, snails and stylised flowers. There is a pronounced crazing of the glaze. 7 inches high, $11\frac{1}{2}$ inches long. c. 1730.

64. A press-moulded tureen standing on three satyr-mask feet, together with a large plate. Both decorated with raised beaded ornament and copied from silver shapes. Plate, 15 inches diameter, Tureen, 6 inches high. c. 1730.

65. A press-moulded tureen and cover standing on three grotesque animal-mask feet (formerly in the collection of Enoch Wood) and three oval moulded plates with matching design of dot, diaper, star and basket pattern in relief. Tureen, 9 inches high. Plates, 13 inches, 15 inches, and 17 inches at greatest width. c. 1730.

66. A press-moulded sugar caster and a tall candlestick decorated with seed pattern in low relief. Such forms were copied from silver prototypes. Candlestick, $10\frac{1}{4}$ inches high. c. 1730.

67. Two white cream-jugs, each standing on three mask and claw feet flanking a greyish-white bowl. The decoration has been applied, using metal dies, and the jugs bear traces of gilding. Cream jug on left, $4\frac{1}{4}$ inches high. c. 1730.

68. A pair of greyish-white vases with applied grape and vine-leaf decoration (page 40). $7\frac{1}{4}$ inches high. c.1730.

69. A particularly interesting water-bottle with trellis, star, five-dot cluster and feather-moulded decoration (page 41). The neck has been thrown and the lower globular portion press-moulded in three conjoined sections. The base has also been made separately. At a later date, bottles were made entirely from moulds. 8 inches high. c. 1735.

70. Two varieties of puzzle-jug (page 41) decorated with horizontal rouletted lines. The one on the right, dated 1735, has a frieze of applied motifs in iron-brown. Both jugs exhibit an overall surface scum, no doubt due to having been fired in a dirty oven. $7\frac{1}{4}$ inches high. c. 1735.

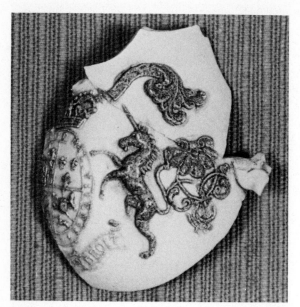

71. A fragment of a rare type of stoneware (page 41) with the royal coat-of-arms applied in clay which has been stained blue. Excavated in Sneyd Green, Stoke-on-Trent, during 1958. 2¾ inches high. c. 1735.

72. A small teapot on moulded tripod feet (page 41), decorated with an applied rose, leaf and fleur-de-lys ornament in blue-stained clay. The plain handle and spout are an early feature. 3¼ inches high. c. 1735.

73. An extremely rare lathe-turned unhandled cup (page 42). The brown (Staffordshire) body has an interior wash of white pipe-clay slip, noticeably whiter below the rim. Ascribed by tradition to John Astbury of Shelton (1688–1743). 3 inches high. c. 1730.

74. A unique punch-bowl which can be identified from the Ralph Shaw patent of 1732 (page 42). This Cobridge, Stoke-on-Trent, potter described his products 'whose outside will be of a true chocolate colour, striped with white, and the inside white, much resembling the brown China ware, and glazed with salt'. In 1736 Shaw sued John Mitchell of Burslem for infringing his patent. 6¼ inches high. 10 inches rim diameter. c. 1735.

75. A selection of hollow-ware fragments excavated in Greenhead
Street, Burslem, during 1964 (page 39). Note the toy coffee-pot.
Mugs, $3\frac{3}{4}$ inches high. 1730–40.

76. A fine thrown and lathe-turned tankard with rim mounted in silver. 7¾ inches high. 4½ inches diameter. c. 1740.

77. A large undecorated thrown and lathe-turned punch-pot with an unusual matt finish. 9¾ inches high. c. 1740.

78. A plain thrown and turned porringer which was excavated on a site adjoining the Albion Hotel, Hanley, during 1966. 2½ inches high. c. 1740+.

79. An undecorated lathe-turned teapot with notched handle (page 42) made by Thomas and John Wedgwood of the Big House, Burslem. In their sales-account book there are references to 'white natched [sic] teapots'. $4\frac{1}{4}$ inches high. c. 1740.

80. A thrown teapot standing on tripod mask feet. The lower portion has panels of incised line decoration above which are applied floral reliefs. Moulded spout and fish handle; lid surmounted by Chinese lion. Traces of gilding. 6 inches high. c. 1740.

81. A rare tankard with turned and incised decoration (page 43). Below the rim are floral emblems, a lion, a unicorn and a royal crown applied with clay taken from metal dies. Note the impressed die impressions. $6\frac{1}{2}$ inches high. c. 1740.

82. A cast documentary teapot (page 32) commemorating the capture of Portobello by Admiral Vernon inscribed 'The Vessel that Admiral Vernon was in at taking Porto Bello, The Burford'. (The lid is a lead-glazed replacement.) 7 inches high. c. 1740.

83. A pair of grey-white bell-shaped potting-pots (page 43) with applied lion masks and festoons of conjoined fruit and flowers. As late as 1785 John Wood, potter of Brownhills, Burslem, was selling '2 Round covered potting pots, Lyons faces, 2/4d'. (An enamelled example is in the Cleveland Museum of Art.) $5\frac{1}{2}$ inches high. c. 1740.

84. A selection of toys (page 44) made by Thomas and John Wedgood of the Big House, Burslem; the handled specimen at the rear is dated 1743. The hollow-ware miniatures illustrate the skill of the thrower, the smallest bowl being only $\frac{3}{4}$ of an inch high. c. 1743+.

85. A rare perforated pomade box and cover. $1\frac{3}{4}$ inches high. c. 1740. *The Metropolitan Museum of Art: gift of Mrs. Russell S. Carter, 1945.*

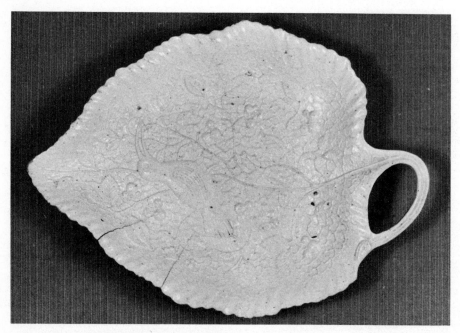

86. A press-moulded leaf dish decorated with a bird on branches eating berries. Similar examples are known in lead-glazed earthenware and attributed to Thomas Whieldon. $11\frac{1}{8}$ inches long. c. 1740.

87. A cast teapot of ribbed pattern (page 44) with a rolled clay handle and a base which has been separately applied. Manufactured by Thomas and John Wedgwood of the Big House, Burslem. $4\frac{1}{4}$ inches high. c. 1745.

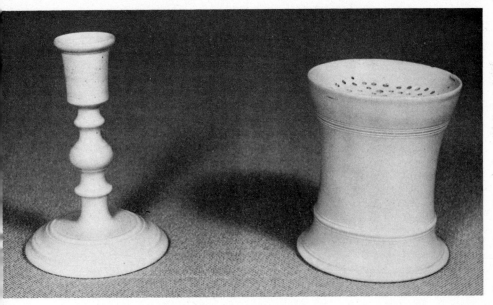

88. A thrown and turned low candlestick and a pounce-pot (sand-sprinkler) made by Thomas and John Wedgwood of the Big House, Burslem (page 43). An interesting feature of the candlestick is that it is white-dipped and the upper section is translucent. Candlestick, $4\frac{1}{2}$ inches high. c. 1745.

89. A block and a cast house-teapot bearing the Arms of England on one side and the Arms of Holland on the reverse. Note the nude figure riding astride the teapot spout (pages 42, 44 and 45). The handle is notched—characteristic of pots made by Thomas and John Wedgwood of the Big House, Burslem. The block came to the City Museum, Stoke-on-Trent, from descendants of these brothers. Block, 5 inches high. c. 1745.

90. A cast house-teapot bearing the Arms of England on one side and the Arms of Holland on the reverse (pages 42, 44 and 45). This variation on a popular theme is picked out in cobalt. Note the notched handle, typical of ware made by Thomas and John Wedgwood of the Big House Burslem. $5\frac{1}{2}$ inches high. c. 1745.

91. A less ornate version of a cast house-teapot (page 45) but unusual because of the bird-chimney and shaped handle. $6\frac{1}{2}$ inches high. c. 1745.

92. Two cast teapots and a block decorated with shells and oak-leaves in relief. The tripod teapot has mask and claw feet. Block, 4 inches high. c. 1745.

93. A pair of cast toy tea-kettles (page 45) with floral decoration in relief. Though damaged, these have been included to show an uncommon form of Staffordshire salt-glaze. The toy with handle, $4\frac{1}{4}$ inches high. c. 1745.

94. A block and two cast heart-shaped teapots ornamented with grapes and vine leaves in relief (pages 42 and 44). The teapot on the left was formerly in the Enoch Wood Collection and the block was made for Thomas and John Wedgwood of the Big House, Burslem. Note the notched handles. Each $4\frac{1}{2}$ inches high. c. 1745.

. A fine cast teapot with
cten shell ornament in relief
ge 45). This decoration on tea-
re was one of the most popular
affordshire productions. 6 inches
jh. c. 1745+.

96. A block and a cast teapot divided into eight panels of grotesque
figures, birds and animals in relief (pages 42 and 44). Note the notched
handle. The block belonged to Thomas and John Wedgwood of the
Big House, Burslem. Block, $4\frac{1}{2}$ inches high. Teapot, 6 inches high.
c. 1745+.

97. A pitcher saucer block (page 30) and a moulded saucer decorated in eight panels with fabulous beasts and birds, including a unicorn and a double-headed eagle in relief. In one compartment, two women are seated at a table partaking of a meal. Block, $5\frac{1}{4}$ inches diameter. Saucer, $4\frac{7}{8}$ inches diameter. c. 1745.

98. A fine cast bowl, teacup and cream-jug (pages 42 and 44) with panels of grotesque figures, birds and animals in relief. Note the notched handle on the cream-jug. Made by Thomas and John Wedgwood of the Big House, Burslem. Bowl, 4 inches high. Cream-jug, 6 inches high. c. 1745.

99. An extremely fine cast bowl divided into eight panels of grotesque figures, birds and animals in relief (page 44). The raised ornament is touched with blue. Made by Thomas and John Wedgwood of the Big House, Burslem. $2\frac{3}{4}$ inches high. c. 1745.

100. A small cast bowl and a block ornamented with pecten shell and scrolls in relief (page 44). Made by Thomas and John Wedgwood of the Big House, Burslem. 3 inches high. c. 1745.

101. A cast cup and a block for a tea-bowl with ribbed and pendant ornament in relief. Lack of definition on the cup indicates that it was made in a worn plaster-of-Paris mould (page 32). Cup, 3 inches high. Block, $2\frac{1}{4}$ inches high. c. 1745.

102. 'The seven Champions of Christendom' bowl. One of the finest examples of the casting process (page 45) in existence. The upright panels of standing figures are labelled, 'St. David Wales', 'St George', 'Denis Fre', 'St. James Spaine', St. Antony Ity', 'St. Andrew Scot', and 'St. Patrick Ired'. The base was made in a separate mould and joined to the upper section with slip. $7\frac{1}{4}$ inches high, $10\frac{3}{8}$ inches diameter. c. 1745. *Colonial Williamsburg.*

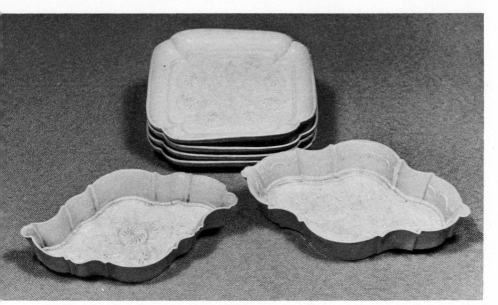

103. A nest of four press-moulded 'square pettys' and two press-moulded 'flowered Spoon boats' (pages 30, 32 and 44). Made by Thomas and John Wedgwood of the Big House, Burslem (descriptions are taken from their crate-book in the City Museum, Stoke-on-Trent). Pettys, $5\frac{1}{2}$ inches square. c. 1745.

104. A pitcher block and a nest of four press-moulded triangular pickle trays ornamented in sharp relief (pages 30 and 44). On one side a crowned head faces to the right. Made by Thomas and John Wedgwood of the Big House, Burslem. Sides of trays, $5\frac{1}{10}$ inches long. c. 1745.

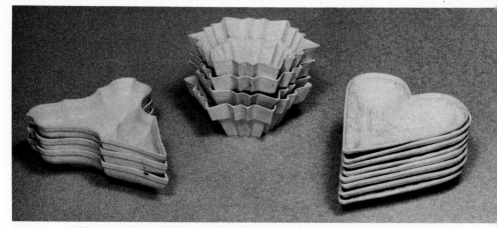

105. A nest of three cast pickle or sweetmeat trays, a nest of four cast 'double-star pettys' and a nest of eight press-moulded 'heart pickle plates' (page 44). The centre and right-hand nests made by Thomas and John Wedgwood of the Big House, Burslem (descriptions are taken from their crate-book in the City Museum, Stoke-on-Trent). Double star petty, 4 inches wide. c. 1745.

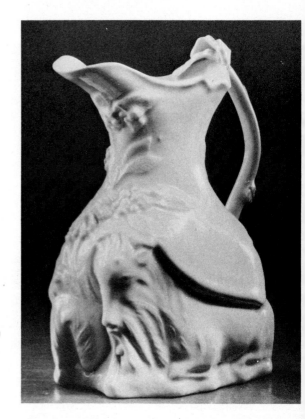

106. A rare cast goat-and-bee jug copied from Chelsea porcelain (page 45). 3¾ inches high. c. 1745–50. *Nelson Gallery, Atkins Museum (gift of Mr. and Mrs. Frank P. Burnap), Kansas City, Missouri.*

107. Three cast shells (page 44) made by Thomas and John Wedgwood of the Big House, Burslem, who record many references to shells both in their sales-account book and crate-book. In 1868 the larger-size ones were selling at 2½p each. Larger shells, 6½ inches long. c. 1745+.

108. A pair of cast 'Turk's Caps', each incised 'CM 1746', flanking a block (page 44). Jelly, blancmange or pudding from such a mould would appear swirled like a turban, hence the name. Made by Thomas and John Wedgwood of the Big House, Burslem, who in 1771 were selling 'Turk's Caps' at 2½p each. Block, 2½ inches high. 1746.

109. A small cast vase, two cast tea-bowls and a block for a teapot ornamented with shell and key-border pattern in relief. Block, 4½ inches high. Tea-bowls, 2 inches high. c. 1750.

110.   A finely cast cream-jug and block with pecten shell and snail ornament in relief (pages 42 and 44). Note the notched handle. A similar block in the Victoria and Albert Museum is incised 'RW 1749'. The cream-jug was made by Thomas and John Wedgwood of the Big House, Burslem. Cream-jug, $4\frac{3}{4}$ inches high. c. 1750.

111.   A block for a coffee-pot and a cast cream-jug with pecten shell and snail ornament in relief. Block, $6\frac{1}{2}$ inches high. Cream-jug, $3\frac{1}{2}$ inches high. c. 1750.

112. Two small cast cream-jugs and a pitcher block (impressed
'LONDON') with Chinese figure subjects and floral border in relief.
Similar cream-jugs are known in lead-glazed earthenware. Block, $3\frac{1}{2}$
inches high. c. 1750.

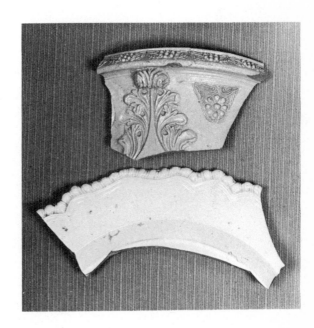

113. Two fragments excavated
on the site of Longton Hall during
1955 (page 41). The upper sherd
is an unusual type of grey stoneware; the lower is a common
white variety with beaded rim. c.
1750.

114. A thrown milk-jug with rouletted zig-zag pattern on handle.
Excavated in Pall Mall, Hanley, during 1954. 8 inches high. c. 1750.

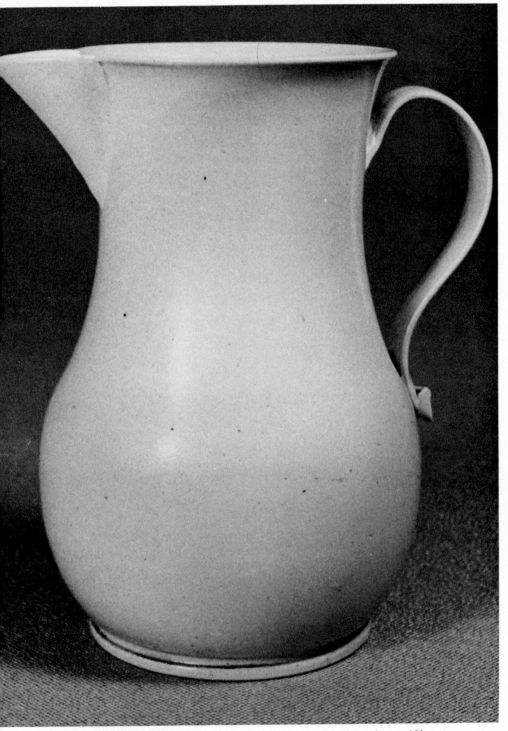

115. An excellent example of a thrown and turned milk-jug (page 43)
which weighs only 8¾ ounces. Made by Thomas and John Wedgwood
of the Big House, Burslem. 7 inches high. c. 1750.

116. Two cylindrical tankards. The one on the right with a heavily pitted glaze was excavated from a site adjoining the Victoria Hall, Hanley, during 1966. The banded specimen is $5\frac{1}{4}$ inches high. c. 1750.

117. A slabbed and pressed double and single tea-caddy (page 45). The double caddy has a bird on a tree within a scroll in relief, and the single caddy has applied rosettes, crown and the impressed initials 'GT' (? Green Tea). Double caddy, $5\frac{3}{4}$ inches high. c. 1750.

118.   A press-moulded single and double white salt-glazed tea-caddy decorated with raised star and five-dot clusters within panels. Shown with a coloured lead-glazed double tea-caddy of similar decoration. Fragments of both type were excavated during 1969 at Fenton Vivian on the site of Thomas Whieldon's manufactory (page 45). Centre caddy, 4 inches high. c. 1750.

119.   A press-moulded white salt-glazed tea-caddy and a coloured lead-glazed teapot ornamented with a Chinaman and a bird in relief. There is proof, from excavations during 1969 at Fenton Vivian (page 45), that Thomas Whieldon manufactured ware bearing the subject. Caddy, 3½ inches high. c. 1750.

120. A press-moulded tile with ornament in relief reputed to have come from a fire-place in Thomas Whieldon's house, The Grove, Fenton Vivian (page 46). $4\frac{7}{8}$ inches square. c. 1750. *The Metropolitan Museum of Art: gift of Mrs. Russell S. Carter, 1945.*

121. A portion of a bottle-cooler with dolphin handles excavated during 1969 on the site of the Thomas Whieldon factory, Fenton Vivian (page 41.) A complete example formerly belonging to Enoch Wood is in the Victoria and Albert Museum. $7\frac{1}{2}$ inches high. c. 1750.

122. A moulded butter-dish stand (page 47) with dot and diaper, star and diaper and basket pattern in relief. 6½ inches long. c. 1750.

123. A moulded fruit dish with panels of seed ornament in relief. Formerly in the Enoch Wood Collection. Note that this shape was later known as 'Queen's shape' (James and Chas. Whitehead pattern book, 1798). 11 inches diameter. c. 1750+.

124. A moulded soup dish with beaded edge and plain panels on rim.
9 inches diameter. c. 1750+.

125. A moulded octagonal plate with a trellis design in relief around
the rim, and a plate with scalloped edge of similar moulded decoration.
The round plate is 9 inches in diameter. c. 1750.

126. A fine press-moulded teapot (page 47), with overlapping leaf decoration in relief, standing on three lion-mask feet. The distinctive rustic handle is rare. $5\frac{1}{2}$ inches high. c. 1750.

127. A rare cast sauce-boat with grotesque animals, fabulous birds, flowers and shells in relief. $3\frac{1}{4}$ inches high. c. 1750.

128. Two cast sauce-boats of silver shape, the example on the left having a horizontal band of hob-nail pattern in relief. Example on the left, $3\frac{1}{2}$ inches high, $9\frac{1}{2}$ inches long. c. 1750.

129. On the left and right a cast sauce-boat, and a press-moulded sauce-boat in the centre, all with ornament in relief. The interior of each flanking specimen shows the typical indentations associated with the casting process (pages 31 and 44). Centre sauce-boat, 3 inches high, $7\frac{1}{2}$ inches long. c. 1750.

130. A small cast sauce-boat with decoration in low relief, and two press-moulded sauce-boats with seed pattern in low relief and scrolls below lip in high relief. Centre sauce-boat, $3\frac{1}{4}$ inches high, $6\frac{3}{4}$ inches long. c. 1750.

131. Three cast twin-handled, double-spouted sauce-boats (page 44) with relief ornament. In the Thomas and John Wedgwood crate-book for 20th Sept. 1770 is the following entry:

6 larg two han^l.   Dyll Sause boats ⎫
8 less   do   one handle   ⎬ 4.7
                                   ⎭

Centre sauce-boat, $3\frac{1}{2}$ inches high, $7\frac{1}{2}$ inches long. c. 1750+.

132. A press-moulded fish and a press-moulded tray ornamented with a Chinese building and figures in relief (page 44). The sales-account book of Thomas and John Wedgwood of the Big House, Burslem, contains several references to 'fishes'. Fish, 7 inches long. Tray, $4\frac{1}{2}$ inches long. c. 1750+.

133. A press-moulded moon and a press-moulded sun made by Thomas and John Wedgwood of the Big House, Burslem (page 44). There are many references in their sales-account book and crate-book in the City Museum, Stoke-on-Trent, to moons and suns. Sun, 4 inches diameter. c. 1750+.

134. Three cast melon jelly moulds. From the sales-account book and crate-book kept by Thomas and John Wedgwood of the Big House, Burslem (page 44), ten sizes of melon were being manufactured and sold from 5p per dozen to 35p per dozen. Centre melon, $4\frac{1}{2}$ inches long. c. 1750.

135. A pleasing and rare fluted cup manufactured by the casting process (page 44) made by Thomas and John Wedgwood of the Big House, Burslem. 2 inches high. c. 1750.

136. Three press-moulded butter-tubs moulded in low relief with trellis work enclosing stars and dots surmounted by a cow cover (page 47). A similar cover in unglazed biscuit earthenware was excavated during 1969 on the Thomas Whieldon factory site at Fenton Vivian, Stoke-on-Trent. Centre tub, $4\frac{1}{2}$ inches high, $5\frac{1}{2}$ inches long. c. 1750.

137. A cast and white dipped 'spitting-pot' with panels of quatrefoil surrounding a pecten shell in relief. In the sales-account book and crate-book kept by Thomas and John Wedgwood of the Big House, Burslem, 'Spitting-pots' are recorded in the 1750s. In 1770 they were being sold for 14p per dozen (page 37). The glaze has crazed on this specimen, 3 inches high. c. 1750+

138. A cast and white-dipped vase with overlapping leaves and a dolphin mask in relief (page 37). As with all such specimens bearing an engobe, the glaze is crazed. The form is also known in porcelain. $7\frac{1}{2}$ inches high. c. 1755.

139. A unique collection of press-moulded table-spoons and tea-spoons made by Thomas and John Wedgwood of the Big House, Burslem (page 44). Their sales-account book and crate-book contain very many references to spoons of all descriptions, including 'holed, unholed, pierced and plain'. Table-spoons, $7\frac{1}{4}$ inches long. Tea-spoons, $5\frac{3}{4}$ inches long. c. 1755+.

140. A unique collection of press-moulded 'holed' and 'plain' table-spoons made by Thomas and John Wedgwood of the Big House, Burslem (pages 30 and 44). From their sales-account book in 1766, '12 Holed Table, 12 Tea spoons' were sold for 15p. In 1769, '6 Doz holed spoons' were sold for 60p. $7\frac{1}{4}$ inches long. c. 1755+.

141. Two moulded plates with raised ornament on the rim (page 47). The example on the left is decorated with multiple cross-pattees within trellis, stylised flower and scroll design (twelve stilt marks on the reverse). The plate on the right is decorated with flower, butterfly, leaf and basket design (sixteen stilt marks on the reverse). 9 inches diameter. c. 1755.

142. A plain and a pierced moulded dessert plate with basket-work, scrolls and fruit in relief. This popular decoration is also known in lead-glazed earthenware. $9\frac{1}{2}$ inches diameter. c. 1755.

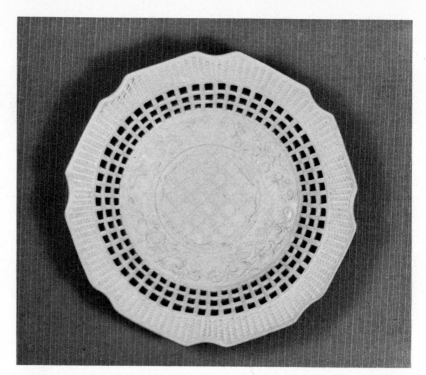

143.   An octagonal moulded and pierced fruit dish with indented angles. In the centre is a basket pattern with scroll border in relief. $8\frac{1}{2}$ inches diameter. c. 1775.

144.   One of the most popular moulded plates ever made (page 47). On the rim, three panels of raised trellis decoration enclose a portrait of the Prussian King, an eagle and trophies of war. Within the plain panels, 'Success to the King of Prussia and his forces' (see Plate 49). $9\frac{1}{2}$ inches diameter. c. 1756.

145.   A cast and white-dipped pierced fruit basket with twisted rope handles and exterior ornament (pages 38 and 41). The glaze has crazed overall but the crackle is particularly pronounced on the base. Compare the production technique with the basket shown in the following illustration. $2\frac{3}{4}$ inches high, 12 inches long. c. 1760.

146.   A rare and intricately pierced fruit basket with moulded flowers, tree and sun motifs sprigged on the inside (page 41). This fine specimen was made by pressing clay into a mould and not by the casting process as is the basket shown in the preceding illustration. $3\frac{1}{4}$ inches high, $13\frac{1}{2}$ inches long. c. 1760.

147. A fine press-moulded dish with scroll and basket work in high and low relief respectively (page 47) with eight panels of pierced trellis work around the rim. This pattern is known in porcelain and lead-glazed earthenware. 13 inches long, 11 inches wide. c. 1760.

148. A pressed and pierced basket and stand with hazel-nut ornament in high relief and basket work in low relief. Stand, 10 inches by $8\frac{1}{2}$ inches. Basket, 9 inches long. c. 1760.

149. A moulded dish covered with raised dot and diaper, star and diaper and basket patterns in scroll-bordered panels. $11\frac{3}{4}$ inches diameter. c. 1760.

150. An oval moulded fruit dish or tureen-stand covered with raised dot and diaper, star and diaper and basket patterns in scroll-bordered panels. One of the most popular productions in salt-glazed stoneware. 12 inches long. c. 1760.

151. A small moulded butter-tub stand with scalloped rim on which is a continuous dot and diaper pattern in relief. This decoration seems to have held favour for the greater part of the white salt-glazed stone-ware period $6\frac{1}{4}$ inches long, 5 inches wide. c. 1760.

*This Dish was Modelled
by Aaron Wood
about the Year 1760,
was Deposited in this Building
AD 1835 by his son Enoch Wood.*

152. An oval moulded documentary dish (page 47) which was deposited in the foundations of the Old Market, Burslem, by the potter Enoch Wood. Enoch had a mania for burying items below public build-ings; and other potters, including Thomas Wedgwood and Samuel Alcock, followed suit. $10\frac{1}{4}$ inches long, $8\frac{1}{4}$ inches wide. c. 1760.

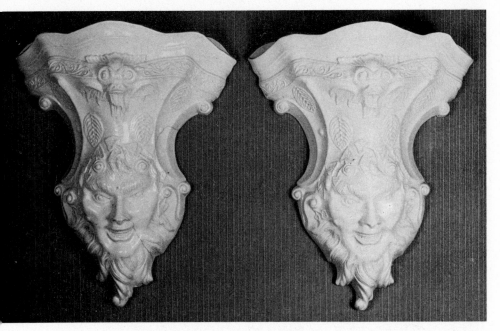

153. A pair of cast satyr wall flower-holders with a dolphin head in relief below the rim. 9 inches long. c. 1760.

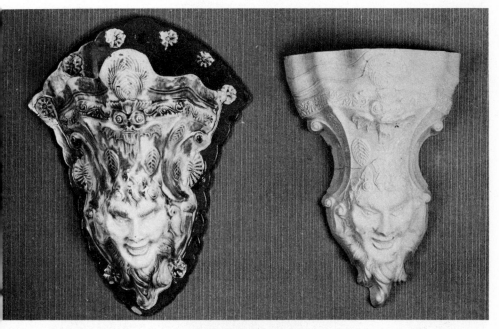

154. A coloured lead-glazed satyr wall flower-holder and a white salt-glazed block shown side by side for comparison. The bearded satyr is crowned with ivy below a dolphin head in relief. Block, $8\frac{1}{2}$ inches long. c. 1760

155. A coloured lead-glazed and white salt-glazed press-moulded mask flower-holder shown side by side for comparison (page 45). As late as December 1770, Thomas and John Wedgwood of the Big House, Burslem, were selling to Richard Franks of Bristol '8 large faces, 6 Midle, 2 least, 8 Flower Horns,.2/– p pair £1. 4. 0'. Lead glazed flower-holder, 13 inches long, c. 1760.

156. A cast wall cornucopia with a bust of Plenty in relief set in a scroll panel (page 45). In the Thomas and John Wedgwood crate-book there is a record of them having sold '10 Corna Copiaes' for 34p in September 1770. 11½ inches long. ç. 1760.

157. A scratch-blue loving cup inscribed 'MB 1748' (page 49) and what possibly may be intended to represent the badge of the Templars or the Agnus Dei flanked with leaf and flower decoration. $6\frac{1}{4}$ inches high. 1748.

158. Two small scratch-blue loving cups flanking a scratch-blue cylindrical tankard (page 50), all with incised floral decoration. Loving cup on the right, 5 inches high. c. 1750.

159. Two scratch-blue cups flanking a scratch-blue tea-bowl (page 50). The two specimens on the left decorated with incised floral motifs and the cup on the right with rouletted decoration in-filled with cobalt. Cups, $2\frac{1}{2}$ inches high. c. 1750.

160. A finely thrown scratch-blue jug with a simple incised floral decoration and a shallow band of rouletting below the rim. (page 50) $5\frac{1}{2}$ inches high. c. 1750.

Above. 161. Two typical scratch-blue jugs with incised flower and leaf decoration (page 50). Very many fragments of this class of ware have been found over the years in the Staffordshire Potteries. Jug on the right, 6¾ inches high. c. 1750. *Right.* 162. A tiny scratch-blue pail (page 50) with scalloped rim, twisted rope handle and simple incised line decoration. 3¼ inches high. c. 1750. *Below.* 163. A scratch-blue bottle and a scratch-blue puzzle jug with the initials 'GW', decorated with floral designs (page 50). Bottle, 8¼ inches high. c. 1750.

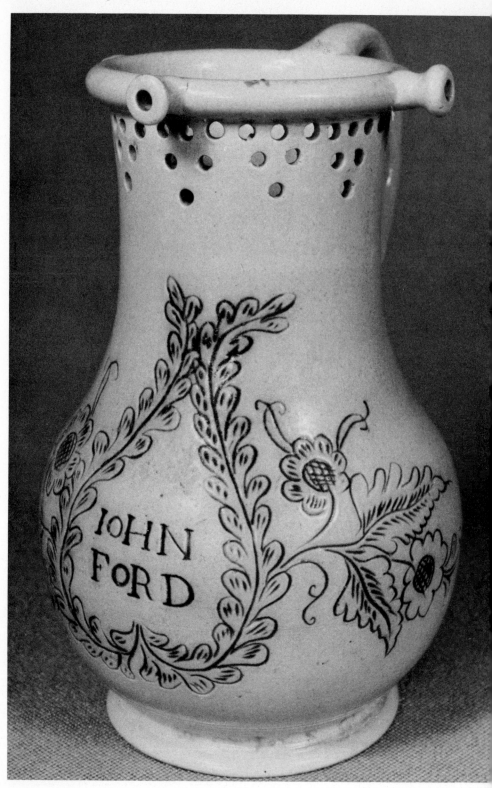

164. A scratch-blue puzzle-jug inscribed 'JOHN FORD' within a panel of incised stylised leaves flanked by incised floral decoration (page 50). $7\frac{1}{4}$ inches high. c. 1750.

165. A large scratch-blue cylindrical mug decorated with incised flowing floral motifs (page 50). The spreading foot is characteristic on squat forms. $7\frac{1}{2}$ inches high. c. 1750.

166. A fine scratch-blue loving-cup inscribed 'EB 1754' (page 49) with incised floral decoration and a narrow band of rouletting below the lathe-turned rim. By tradition, this example is attributed to Enoch Booth of Tunstall, Stoke-on-Trent. $7\frac{1}{4}$ inches high. 1754.

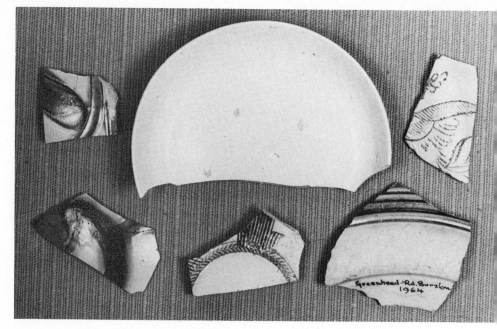

167. A selection of scratch-blue and white salt-glazed fragments excavated at various sites in Burslem (page 50). Saucer, $4\frac{1}{2}$ inches in diameter. c. 1740–70.

168. A selection of scratch-blue tavern ware made during the earlier part of George III's reign (page 50) with applied 'GR' and crown stamps. The fragment was excavated during 1967 in Nile Street, Burslem. Centre jug, $5\frac{1}{2}$ inches high. c. 1760+.

169. A scratch-blue flask inscribed 'BENGAMIN MELLOR 1775' (page
50) with a band of incised floral decoration around the edge. In the
British Museum there is a smaller version decorated in scratch-brown
dated 1724, which indicates that flasks were decorated in this manner
for half a century. 6 inches in diameter. 1775.

170. An elegant Littler-Wedgwood blue coffee-pot and cover (pages 52 and 59) with floral gilding. Jonah Malkin in his sales-account book (City Museum, Stoke-on-Trent) records that he purchased on the 10th September 1749, 'Japand flowred new coller from Aaron Wedg^wd'. Elsewhere in the accounts this ware is referred to as 'Aaron's blue'. 8½ inches high. c. 1750.

171. A rare Littler-Wedgwood blue wall tile (page 52) with moulded pecten shell pattern in relief. The tile is made in two flat sections, the blue being laid on a thin white-clay bat which is backed with a thicker slab made from suggar-marl. $5\frac{1}{4}$ inches square. c. 1750.

172. A Littler-Wedgwood blue teapot with crabstock handle and spout, bird finial on cover and three mask and claw feet (page 53). In the Thomas and John Wedgwood papers (City Museum, Stoke-on-Trent), references are made to 'Cusen Aaron Wedgwood' in association with 'Blew teapots'. $3\frac{3}{4}$ inches high. c. 1750+.

173.   A Littler-Wedgwood blue vase and teapot with cover (page 53). The vase is of Chinese shape and the teapot has a crabstock handle and spout. Vase, $6\frac{1}{4}$ inches high. Teapot, $4\frac{1}{2}$ inches high. c. 1750+.

174.   A superb Littler-Wedgwood blue teapot painted in white enamel (page 53). Such rare and choice examples show the excellent marriage between the skills of the potter and decorator. $4\frac{3}{4}$ inches high. c. 1750. *David E. Zeitlin Collection, Merion, Pennsylvania.*

175. A rare tankard with a full-length gilded portrait of Prince Charles Edward Stuart (pages 58 and 60), flanked by a rose and a thistle. Inscribed below the rim 'The Next Spring restore the King' and above the base 'Down with the Rump'. A tankard with similar decoration inscribed 'God Bless Prince C. Stuart' is in the Burnap Collection, Kansas City. $5\frac{1}{8}$ inches high. c. 1745. *The Metropolitan Museum of Art: gift of Mrs Russell S. Carter, 1945.*

176.　A small, rare straight-sided teapot with crabstock handle and spout and twig finial on cover (page 58) with buildings and landscape enamelled in brown, pink, pale blue, green and yellow. $2\frac{3}{4}$ inches high. c. 1750. *The Metropolitan Museum of Art: gift of R. Thornton Wilson, 1937.*

177.　A rare teapot standing on three shell feet with plain handle and spout. On one side a kneeling man in tartan breeches holds an uplifted glass of wine above the word 'KING' and on the reverse a man drinking wine above the word 'IOB'. Enamelled in puce, green, yellow, blue and black. $3\frac{1}{2}$ inches high. c. 1750.

178. A lobed cast teapot and cover (page 58) with oak-leaves, acorns and overlapping pecten shells in relief, and lid surmounted by a Chinese lion. Around the base and on the neck is a raised key border. Flowers, trailing stems and two small busts are painted in enamel colours. 6 inches high. c. 1750.

179. A small teapot with plain handle and spout decorated with buildings and landscapes in polychrome enamels, and a teapot and cover with crabstock handle and spout decorated with a bird amidst foliage in polychrome enamels. Covered teapot, $3\frac{3}{4}$ inches high. c. 1750–60.

180. A fine pair of cups decorated with a man playing a flute, and a coffee-pot decorated with figures set against a landscape. All three in bright polychrome enamels (page 59). A creamware coffee-pot with a similar moulded spout and decoration is known. Cups, $2\frac{1}{2}$ inches high. Coffee-pot, $9\frac{1}{2}$ inches high. c. 1755.

181. A choice and extremely rare toy teapot and cover (page 58) with a rose and rose-leaves enamelled in red, green and yellow on a black enamelled ground. The Thomas and John Wedgwood crate-book (City Museum, Stoke-on-Trent) contains references to 'Toy tea pots'. $2\frac{1}{2}$ inches high. c. 1755.

182. A press-moulded teapot and cover with crabstock handle and spout and bi-valve shell finial. Painted in red and green enamels with handle and spout in green, yellow shell finial. $3\frac{7}{8}$ inches high. c. 1755. *The Metropolitan Museum of Art: gift of Carleton Macy, 1934.*

183. A fine moulded teapot and cover (page 58) with eight panels depicting various military subjects in relief, and crabstock handle and spout. Enamelled in blue, pink, yellow and green. Similar rabbit finials were found during 1969 in excavations at Fenton Vivian on the site of Thomas Whieldon's post-1747 factory site. 5 inches high. c. 1755. *Colonial Williamsburg.*

184. A unique enamelled presentation jug (page 56) inscribed 'J. Walter de Checkley, 1760—to every creature was a Friend'. In his hand, a book entitled 'Art of Farriery', and on each side of the portrait panel, sprays of flowers in red, pink, yellow, blue, green and black enamel. Made by the Reverend John Middleton (1714–1802) of Shelton, Stoke-on-Trent. For details on base, see following illustration. 7 inches high.

185. Inscription on the base of the enamelled John Walter de Checkley jug (page 56) made by the Reverend John Middleton, who was Curate of Hanley from 1737–1802 and partner of the potter Warner Edwards of Shelton. See preceding illustration. $3\frac{1}{8}$ inches diameter. Dated 1760.

186.   A block and sauce-boat (page 59) with trellis and scroll pattern
in relief. The sauce-boat is enamelled in brilliant green, blue, red and
yellow. Similar specimens are known in Longton Hall porcelain. Sauce-
boat, $6\frac{1}{2}$ inches long. c. 1755.

187.   Two small teapots and covers, each with crabstock handle and
spout (page 58). The example on the left is enamelled with a female
figure in a landscape within a panel and leaf scrolls in black enamel
on a green ground, and reddish-brown handle and spout. The teapot
on the right has a green and black enamelled net ground and, within
a panel, the bust of Frederick King of Prussia enamelled in red, blue,
green and brown. $3\frac{1}{2}$ inches high. c. 1760.

188. A moulded plate with star, basket-work and dot pattern between scrolls on the rim and a portrait of Frederick the Great decorated in polychrome enamels. $9\frac{1}{2}$ inches diameter. c. 1756. *Colonial Williamsburg.*

189. A miniature cream-jug, tea-bowl and saucer (pages 58 and 59) decorated with floral designs in Chinese style in red, green and yellow enamels. Cream-jug, $2\frac{3}{4}$ inches high. Saucer, $4\frac{1}{2}$ inches diameter. c. 1760.

190. A moulded plate with raised flowers and leaves around the rim and a rural landscape with figures in the foreground below a duplicated 'TH' monogram (page 58). Enamelled in red, green, yellow and black. $9\frac{1}{8}$ inches in diameter. c. 1760.

191. A rare jug bearing an unidentified coat-of-arms (page 59) between floral sprays in the Chinese style painted in polychrome enamels. $9\frac{3}{4}$ inches high. c. 1760.

192.   A very rare moulded plate (page 58) with perhaps the most favoured type of raised decoration around the rim. The Chinese scene is painted with a combination of polychrome enamels and gilding on a black enamel ground. The underside is enamelled in green. 10½ inches in diameter. c. 1760.

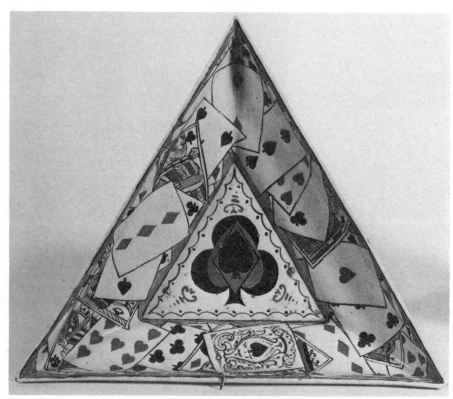

193.   A rare press-moulded triangular enamelled card tray. One card bears the initials 'WT'. 8⅝ inches high. c. 1760. *The Metropolitan Museum of Art: gift of Carleton Macy, 1937, in memory of his wife, Helen Lefferts Macy.*

194. Two teapots with cover, each with crabstock handle and spout. the floral one on the left is enamelled in red, green, yellow, blue and lilac; the example on the right is enamelled in purple/brown to simulate fossil forms as found in limestone, and the flower-finial is enamelled in red and blue (page 58). Teapot on the right, $4\frac{1}{2}$ inches high. c. 1760.

195. A choice teapot and cover with crabstock handle and spout; roses and rose-buds in red enamel on an enamelled blue ground. $4\frac{3}{4}$ inches high. c. 1760.

196.   Two small teapots with cover (page 58), each with a crabstock
handle and spout. The example on the left shows, within a panel, a
house and landscape enamelled in black, dark-green, yellow and blue
against a pink enamelled ground. The teapot on the right is decorated
with feather-like scrolls in green, yellow, blue and red; turquoise
handle and spout. Scroll teapot, $3\frac{1}{4}$ inches high. c. 1760.

197.   Two teapots with cover (page 58), each with crabstock handle
and spout. The example on the left has a floral decoration enamelled
in pink, green and yellow on a brown scale ground. The teapot on the
right has sprays of flowers enamelled in pink on a brown net ground
with handle and spout in green enamel. Teapot on the right, 5 inches
high. c. 1760.

198. On the left, a fine jug decorated with Chinese-style figures, flowers and leaves in polychrome enamels, and a larger jug with floral decoration enamelled in a bold and rather careless manner. Details on both specimens are outlined in black enamel (page 58). Larger jug, $6\frac{3}{4}$ inches high. c. 1760.

199. A large and splendid jug (pages 58 and 59) bearing the Arms of Walthall of Wistaston and Leek (Staffordshire) and landscapes, dragonfly and moths in polychrome enamels. All details are outlined in black enamel. 12 inches high. c. 1760.

200. Two fine teapots and cover, each with crabstock handle and spout (page 58), decorated in Chinese style with brilliant red, yellow, green and blue enamels. Teapot on left, $4\frac{1}{4}$ inches high. c. 1760.

201. Two extremely fine mugs, beautifully decorated in Chinese style (page 58) in polychrome enamels, flanking a teapot and cover with crabstock handle and spout also enamelled with Chinese subjects. The two mugs were made by Thomas and John Wedgwood of the Big House, Burslem. Jug on the left, 5 inches high. c. 1760.

202. A fine jug (page 58) decorated with a continuous landscape
containing trees, a house, and a man and woman walking. Red, blue
and green enamels predominate, with clouds in pink and blue. 8 inches
high. c. 1760.

203. A superb jug (page 58) with an exotic bird on a branch above clusters of berries enamelled in purple, brick red, yellow and green. All details are outlined in black enamel. 5 inches high. c. 1760.

204. A unique vase decorated with flowers, leaves, butterflies, winged insects, a caterpillar and crabs painted in dull green, brick red, yellow, black and blue enamels, with a small amount of size-gilding (page 58). 5 inches high. c. 1760.

205. A straight-sided cup with floral decoration; a cream-jug and cover depicting a man playing a pipe; and, on the right, a beaker of unusual form decorated with a house and landscape. All three painted in polychrome enamels. Beaker, 4 inches high. c. 1760.

206. A fine bowl with polychrome enamel floral decoration in the Chinese style (page 58) and a narrow band of trellis and panels on the inside rim. $3\frac{3}{4}$ inches high, $9\frac{1}{2}$ inches diameter. c. 1760.

207. Three fine mugs in polychrome enamels (page 58) decorated in Chinese style. On the left, a bird in flight amidst flowers and branches; in the centre, floral designs with a rose tied with a ribbon; on the right, a bird on a rock flanked by floral sprays. Mug on the right, 5 inches high. c. 1760.

208. Three jugs with typical handles and spouts decorated in the Chinese style with polychrome enamels. Jug on the right, 6½ inches high. c. 1760.

209. A unique jug inscribed 'James & Martha Jinkeuson 1764' (page 58). The rich enamelled flowers and insects are well painted Dated specimens are rare. 6½ inches high. 1764.

210. A fine moulded teapot and cover (page 59) with polychrome enamels modelled by William Greatbatch in 1764. Blocks for this teapot are in the Wedgwood Museum, Barlaston. 5 inches high. c. 1764. *Mrs. Robert D. Chellis, Wellesley Hills, Mass.*

211. A unique punch-bowl on pedestal foot inscribed within a scroll panel 'JC 1767', on either side of which are fine floral sprays in poly-chrome enamels. 8½ inches diameter. 1767. *Colonial Williamsburg.*

212. A moulded plate with a border of stars and dots within a diaper in relief (page 61) and red on-glaze transfer print 'Le Marchand d'Oiseaux' after Boucher, engraved by J. Daullé. (An octagonal plate with another print in this series is in the Cleveland Museum of Art.) 9 inches in diameter. c. 1755.

213. A moulded plate with a border of stars and dots within a diaper in relief (page 62) and a red on-glaze transfer print of the 'Dog in the Manger' from Aesop's fables. In the Thomas and John Wedgwood sales-account book (City Museum, Stoke-on-Trent) they record having received by contra on the 7th September 1767, 'Red copper plate Ewers etc.' 9 inches in diameter, c. 1755.

214.   A moulded plate with a border of stars and dots within a diaper in relief (pages 47 and 61) and an on-glaze purple transfer print of Diana and Endymion. The pockets of minute discoloration on the rim suggest the possibility of the print having been dusted with colour, hence the faded appearance and lack of definition. On the reverse there are twelve stilt marks, and twelve marks can also be seen on the front. $7\frac{1}{4}$ inches in diameter. c. 1755.

215.   A moulded plate with a border of stars and dots with diaper rim in relief (pages 47 and 62) and an on-glaze sepia transfer print of the sacking of the Temple of Diana at Ephesus by Herostratus. The edge is banded in black and there are stilt marks on the front and on the reverse. $7\frac{1}{2}$ inches in diameter. c. 1755. *The Metropolitan Museum of Art: gift of Carleton Macy, 1934.*

216. A fine jug dated 1773 (page 40). The basket of flowers is framed within a scale pattern painted in iron red and green enamels together with gilding. This is one of the latest known dated examples of Staffordshire salt-glazed stoneware. $4\frac{1}{2}$ inches high. 1773.

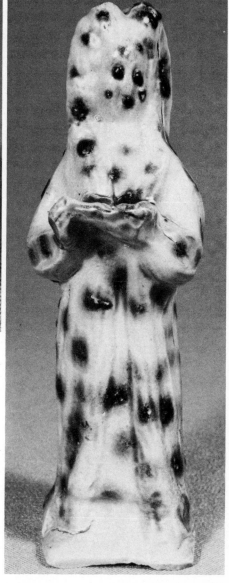

217. A simple press-moulded figure of a woman wearing a wide-hooped flounced skirt with a Watteau pleat on the reverse (page 64). The hollow interior has suggested the possibility of its use as a candle-snuffer. A figure from the same mould is in the Victoria and Albert Museum. 3¾ inches high. c. 1725.

218. A crude grey-white press-moulded figure with cobalt splashes, standing in a long wig and gown, reading from an open book (page 64). Reputed to represent Dr. Henry Sacheverell 1674–1724). 8¾ inches high. c. 1725.

219. A press-moulded figure of a game-cock decorated in iron slip
(pages 64 and 65). Excavated at Broughton Old Hall, Staffordshire.
Similar specimens are in the Macy Collection, Metropolitan Museum of
Art. $4\frac{3}{4}$ inches high. c. 1725.

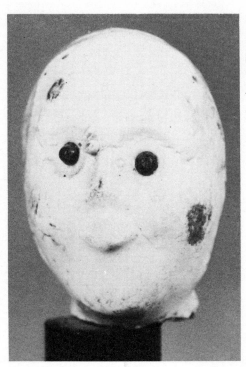

220. A press-moulded bewigged head, with eyes picked out in brown clay. The back of the head is made from brown and white marbled clay. Excavated during 1955 at Longton Hall, Stoke-on-Trent (page 63). 1 inch high. c. 1725.

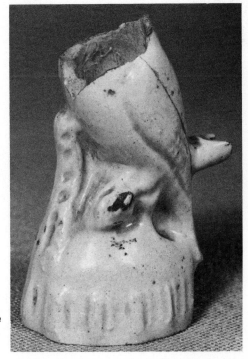

221. A press-moulded fragment of a bird-call excavated in Burslem, Stoke-on-Trent. Note the tail mouth-piece (page 64). 3 inches high. c. 1725.

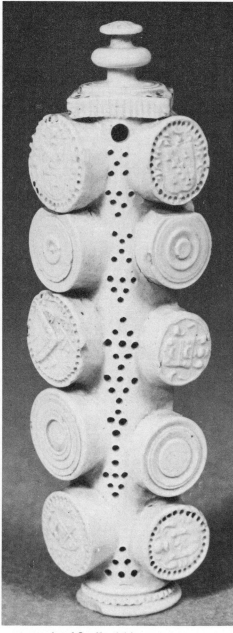

222. Front and rear view of a unique example of Staffordshire press-
moulded and hand-modelled salt-glazed stoneware dated 1732 depicting the Crucifixion (pages 63 and 68). Above the head are the letters
'INRI', and below the feet are a skull, cross-bones, hourglass and bell.
The projections on each side and the nail-marks on the hands and
feet have slight indentations in-filled with brown slip. On the reverse
are four plain and six moulded roundels bearing unidentified coats-of-
arms, between which are groups of small perforations surmounted by
a hole. Made by Aaron Wedgwood or his sons Thomas and John of the
Big House, Burslem, $4\frac{1}{4}$ inches high. 1732.

223. A fine scratch-brown press-moulded figure of a woman (page 66) with hand-modelled arms, hands, bodice and skirt. Details are in brown clay and brown slip. 7¼ inches high. c. 1735. *Colonial Williamsburg.*

224. A press-moulded grotesque dog with stamped ornamentation consisting of crosses, lines and dots. The tail is formed from a section of rolled clay. 4$\frac{3}{8}$ inches high. c. 1735. *The Metropolitan Museum of art: gift of Carleton Macy, 1934.*

225. A fine press-moulded and hand-modelled pew-group (page 65) with a man and a woman seated on a high-backed bench. A fearsome-looking dog separates the couple and the man has a dog sitting between his legs. Above the perforated back is a row of six moulded faces alternating with rosettes. Details in brown clay. 6 inches high, 6¼ inches long. c. 1740. *Nelson Gallery, Atkins Museum (gift of Mr. and Mrs. Frank P. Burnap), Kansas City, Missouri.*

226. A fine press-moulded and hand-modelled pew-group (page 65). The frock-coated men are playing a violin and bagpipes; and the woman, who wears a tight bodice and an apron over a pleated skirt, is holding a lap-dog. Details in brown clay. 6½ inches high, 8 inches long. c. 1740. *Nelson Gallery, Atkins Museum (gift of Mr. and Mrs. Frank P. Burnap), Kansas City, Missouri.*

227. A fine press-moulded
Madonna and Child inspired
by *blanc-de-Chine* figures
of Fukien porcelain (c. 1720)
depicting the Virgin Mary
and child as Kuan Yin
(page 66). A similar example
was later issued in
Staffordshire with coloured
glazes impressed 'VIRGIN
MARY'. 9 inches high.
c. 1740.

228.   A drab-coloured bear-jug covered with shreds of clay to imitate
fur, and dot and line detail in dark brown slip (pages 63 and 65). The
detachable head serves as a drinking cup. Such jugs usually depict a
bear sitting up on its haunches hugging a dog, but in this example the
bear holds a curved whistle (incomplete). 7 inches high. c. 1740.

229. An unusual rattle in the form of a bear hugging a dog (page 65)
manufactured by a combination of throwing and hand-modelling, with
details in dark brown slip. $2\frac{3}{4}$ inches high. c. 1740. *The Metropolitan
Museum of Art: gift of Mrs. Russell S. Carter, 1945.*

230. An outstanding greyish-white figure of a mounted Hussar (page
65) with accoutrements, combining the techniques of press-moulding
and hand-modelling. The horse stands on a press-moulded base which
shows in relief a supine Chinaman. $8\frac{3}{4}$ inches high. c. 1740.

231. A rare press-moulded cow-creamer and calf standing on a rectangular base with scalloped sides (pages 64 and 65). Brown clay is used for the cow's eyes. 5½ inches high. c. 1745.

232. A press-moulded white cat and a press-moulded brown and white solid-agate cat (page 66), both with eyes picked out in brown slip. Both examples are hollow, without bases, and thus of simple manufacture from a two-piece mould. Solid-agate cat, 5 inches high. c. 1745.

233. Two sizes of press-moulded solid-agate cats (page 66) marbled in white and blue clay, with the ears, eyes and body splashes in cobalt. Wads of marbled clay ready for pressing were excavated during the 1920s at Fenton Low, Stoke-on-Trent, on the site of Thomas Whieldon's first factory. Left-hand figure, 4½ inches high. c. 1745.

234. Press-moulded figures of the Duke of Cumberland (also known in Chelsea porcelain) and Queen Anne. The eyes of the Duke are picked out in brown slip and the greyish-white figure of Queen Anne decorated in scratch-blue. Duke 7 inches high. Queen Anne, $7\frac{1}{2}$ inches high. c. 1745.

235. A fine pair of press-moulded horses reclining on simple slab bases decorated with applied leaves and flowers. A similar figure (page 66) in lead-glazed earthenware with Whieldon-type colours is in the City Museum, Stoke-on-Trent. $4\frac{1}{4}$ inches high, $8\frac{1}{2}$ inches long. c. 1745. *Colonial Williamsburg.*

236. A fine and rare press-moulded figure of a doe reclining on a shaped slab base with applied leaf and flower ornament. $3\frac{5}{8}$ inches high, $5\frac{3}{4}$ inches long. c. 1745. *The Metropolitan Museum of Art: gift of Carleton Macy, 1934.*

237. A pair of press-moulded pug-dogs sitting on rectangular slab bases. Similar figures are known in lead-glazed earthenware and in porcelain (pages 63 and 66). Dog on left, 3 inches high. Base, $2\frac{1}{2}$ inches by $1\frac{1}{2}$ inches. c. 1745.

238. A pair of press-moulded Lohans with traces of size-gilding (page 67). Copied from *blanc-de-Chine* figures of Fukien porcelain (c. 1720). $4\frac{1}{4}$ inches high. c. 1745.

239. A press-moulded figure of a shepherd, decorated with touches of cobalt, standing on a perforated pedestal. This popular figure is known in Staffordshire redware and lead-glazed earthenware (pages 63 and 67). Biscuit fragments were found during excavations in Fenton Vivian on the site first occupied by Thomas Whieldon in 1747. $5\frac{1}{8}$ inches high. c.1747.

240. An outstanding pair of musicians in naturalistic attitude, bearing a pronounced similarity to examples in Longton Hall porcelain (pages 63 and 67). Crude leaf and flower ornament decorates the base. Man, $4\frac{3}{4}$ inches high. c. 1750. *The Metropolitan Museum of Art: gift of Carleton Macy, 1937, in memory of his wife, Helen Lefferts Macy.*

241. A rare press-moulded patch-box with screw lid. Similar forms are known in porcelain and in lead-glazed earthenware. 1¾ inches high. c. 1750. *The Metropolitan Museum of Art: gift of Carleton Macy, 1937, in memory of his wife, Helen Lefferts Macy.*

242. A reclining sheep and lamb decorated in enamel colours. Copied from Chelsea porcelain but also known in lead-glazed Staffordshire earthenware (pages 63 and 66). A similar specimen in Whieldon-type colouring is in the Lucy Truman Aldrich Collection, Rhode Island Museum of Art, 3½ inches high. c. 1755. *The Metropolitan Museum of Art: anonymous gift, 1950.*

243.   A pair of rare figures decorated in polychrome enamels and no doubt copied from porcelain originals (page 67). 5 inches high. c. 1755. *The Metropolitan Museum of Art: gift of Carleton Macy, 1934.*

244. Two unique lathe-turned tankards partially covered with a ferruginous wash and bearing an impressed crown and 'WR' cypher. Excavated in the 1930s during alterations to the Crown Staffordshire China factory, Fenton, Stoke-on-Trent. $5\frac{3}{8}$ inches high. c. 1700. *Mr. David W. P. Green, Bagnall, Stoke-on-Trent.* (These important pots came to hand after this book had gone to press, which is why there is no reference to them in the text).

ceremony where the beverage is obviously not tea (Colour Plate III), and the subject of Bacchus astride a barrel (Frontispiece) clearly conveys for what purpose this three-gallon container was used. Punch-pots were therefore made sufficiently large for communal drinking and the smaller teapots for individual needs.

Of rarer form is the coffee pot which normally had a simple moulded spout and a thin strap handle with characteristic lower terminal where the clay was folded back (Colour Plate VII, Plates 170 and 180). The number which has survived is in no way comparable to that of the prolific teapot; most bear enamelled decoration with landscapes, figures or floral subjects. The shape is more or less standard; and examples are known in creamware with the same moulded spout used for salt-glazed coffee pots, such as the specimen in the City Museum and Art Gallery, Stoke-on-Trent (Plate 180).

Originally, teapots and coffee-pots were sold by the Staffordshire potters as part of a service made up of cream-jugs, tea-bowls, saucers, plates, slop-basins and spoon-trays matched in design by the enameller. Two cups painted in bright yellow, red, blue and green within black outlines (Plate 180) and a tea-bowl and saucer enamelled in the Chinese manner (Plate 189) would have been purchased in a complete table-service.

An interesting sauce-boat from a dinner-service (Plate 186) enamelled in brilliant green, blue, red and yellow is in every way similar to known examples made at the Longton Hall porcelain manufactory during its middle period. As previously mentioned, the copying of porcelain shapes in salt-glazed stoneware was by no means uncommon, though it is more noticeable with the plain white ware than with the enamelled.

Chinese heraldic porcelain appears to have influenced the salt-glaze artist in his representation of English coats-of-arms, seen to good effect on the larger jugs (Plate 191). Some arms are difficult to identify, but those of one North Staffordshire family, Walthall of Wistaston and Leek, are clearly intended on a massive jug in the City Museum, Stoke-on-Trent (Plate 199). As with coffee-pots, these large jugs have the typical thinly potted strap-handle and characteristic lower terminal.

While it is unlikely that more than a fraction of enamelled salt-glazed stoneware will ever be satisfactorily linked to a particular painter or manu-facturer, there is occasionally sufficient supporting evidence to give a fairly positive attribution. For example, in 1905 at the Wedgwood Works, Etruria, some crates were discovered containing a collection of eighteenth-century blocks which corresponded to contemporary descriptions given by the modeller William Greatbatch. The following invoice mentions a 'landskip' teapot.

Lane Delf Jany. 11 1764 Mr. Josiah Wedgwood to W^m. Greatbatch
   1 Leaf Candlestick   0 4 0
   1 Oval Fruit basket & Stand   12
   1 p^r CornuCopias   12

F

3 Oblong fruit dishes	3	3
1 Round ditto	1	1
2 Plates do.	2	2
1 Pine Aple Teapot		8 0
Landskip Tpt Saus b^t ⎫		
Cream B^t & Sug^r Box ⎭	1	7
3 Faces		15
1 Chinese Teapots		10 6
	10	14 6
Recd on acc^t of the above	3	3 0
Balance	7	11 6
Received the contents		

The original block can be seen at the Wedgwood factory, Barlaston. A number of landscape teapots based on this model are known in lead-glazed earthenware, creamware and enamelled saltglaze (Plate 210).

From the second quarter of the eighteenth century various forms of gilding were used on Staffordshire salt-glazed stoneware. Like the enamels, gilding was fixed by firing the pots for a second time in a muffle kiln but at a much lower temperature than that required for enamels. As described in the potting trade, it was merely 'hardened on'. A failing of some size-gilding was its impermanence, as illustrated by the 'white-dipped' jug (Plate 57) in the City Museum, Stoke-on-Trent; but certain gilded salt-glaze has survived which shows to good effect the skill of the craftsman in this branch of ceramic decoration. A rare and wonderfully preserved pro-Jacobite mug (Plate 175) in the Metropolitan Museum, New York, bearing a full-length portrait of Prince Charles Edward Stuart flanked by a rose and thistle, has inscribed around the top 'The Next Spring restore the King' and around the bottom 'Down with the Rump'. Another outstanding specimen with the same subject, in the Burnap Collection, Kansas City, is inscribed 'God Bless Prince C. Stuart'. Both these fine examples would have been manufactured in or shortly after 1745 when, despite the ill-fated Rebellion, the 'King over the Water' had his supporters who risked severe penalties imposed by George II and drank in secret to the health of their prince.

Transfer-printing

Another method of decorating white salt-glazed stoneware was the semi-mechanical process of transferring prints from an engraved copper-plate to the pot by means of transfer-papers. Seemingly confined to octagonal and round plates having a moulded rim of stars and dots within a diaper between medallions with foliate borders in relief, transfer-printed stoneware had a short life and was ousted by transfer-printed creamware. The minutely-pitted surface of salt-glaze was not an ideal base for red, purple and sepia prints, which were seen to better effect on the smooth lead-glazed creamware.

Until recently, the credit for the invention of ceramic printing has gone to

John Sadler and Guy Green of Liverpool, who, in their famous affidavit dated 2nd August 1756, claimed that, unaided, they did 'within the space of six hours, to whit, betwixt the hours of nine in the morning and three in the afternoon of the same day, print upwards of twelve hundred tiles of different patterns'. The affidavit also stated that 'they had been upwards of seven years in finding out the method of printing tiles and in making trials and experiments'. This oft-quoted statement should now be compared with the findings of Bernard Watney (*Trans. English Ceramic Circle*, Vol. 6, Pt. 2, 1966, pp. 60–3) who, with Robert Charleston, gave the outstanding papers *Petitions for Patents concerning Porcelain, Glass and Enamels with special reference to Birmingham, 'The Great Toyshop of Europe'*. Here we learn that John Brooks, the Irish engraver, was responsible for three petitions for patents. In the first, dated 10th September 1751, when he was residing in Birmingham, he claimed he was able to transfer-print enamels and china; in the second, dated 25th January 1754, when he was living in Battersea, that he could print on glass, 'stone and earthenware'. To my knowledge, this is the only contemporary reference to the printing of salt-glazed stoneware and it is possible that Brooks was already practising this in Birmingham prior to leaving for Battersea in 1753. I see no reason, therefore, why the North Staffordshire potters working in the 1750s should not have sent plain white salt-glazed plates to Birmingham to be printed on-glaze. Whieldon, Wedgwood, Adams and doubtless many other men from the Potteries had commercial links with this great industrial centre, from whence the news of any ceramic innovation would have come to their notice. We know that vast quantities of undecorated ware from Staffordshire were later despatched to Liverpool for printing in the workshop of Messrs Sadler and Green, but I am suggesting that around the year 1755 nothing would have prevented salt-glazed plates from being sent the forty-three miles from Stoke-on-Trent to Birmingham for transfer-printing.

As mentioned previously, the majority of printed plates have a similar border moulded in relief, octagonal examples having scrolls at the angles—such as the set of eight, each bearing an individual illustration of one of Aesop's fables, in the Victoria and Albert Museum (Schreiber Collection) and the specimen 'Blowing Soap Bubbles' in the Cleveland Museum of Art. Definition is often lacking in some of this early printed ware as can be seen by one plate in the City Museum, Stoke-on-Trent, bearing an on-glaze purple print of Diana and Endymion (Plate 214). Here the minute pockets discolouring the rim suggest the possibility of the print having been dusted with powder colour, using size as the transfer medium. A feature of many plates is the number of 'stilt' marks on the back and front; twelve or more have been noted on one specimen—unusual that so many should have been found necessary to keep the plates apart when stacked during firing.

Contemporary engravings were popular with the printers of salt-glaze, who were sadly lacking in originality. Works after Boucher were a favourite —such as 'Le Marchand d'Oiseaux', which was engraved by J. Daullé and issued by the English printers on white salt-glazed stoneware as a red print

(Plate 212). 'La Marchande d'Oeufs' and 'La Vandangeuse' are also found as prints on salt-glazed plates.

Another of Aesop's fables, the 'Dog in the Manger' (Plate 213) is illustrated as a brick-red print on a nine-inch plate in the City Museum, Stoke-on-Trent. Plates of similar diameter in the fable series include:

    The Frog and the Ox
    The Stag and the Water
    The Mountain in Labour
    The Lion and the Forester
    The Wolf and the Crane
    The Ass and the Boar
    The Lion in Love
    The Countryman and Hercules.

An unusual sepia print on salt-glazed stoneware, in the Metropolitan Museum of Art, appears to represent the sacking of the Temple of Diana at Ephesus by Herostratus (Plate 215). Here again stilt marks are evident, but the black-banded edge is far less common.

No evidence exists to suggest that the Staffordshire potter ever decorated his own salt-glazed ware; once his plates left for the printer's workshop, the potter had no say in the finished product. The marriage between print and pot was obviously not a happy one and lasted only for a short time. On creamware, however, it became an unqualified success and laid the foundations for the vast industry which was later to flood the market with blue-printed earthenware.

Chapter VIII

Salt-glazed Figures

Towards the end of the seventeenth century, when brown salt-glazed stone-ware was making its appearance in North Staffordshire, the majority of potters were manufacturing slipware for the kitchen, dairy and table. At a time when thrown dishes were giving way to moulded ware the earliest Staffordshire figures emerged in the form of animals, produced by pressing clay into a two-piece mould. These toys (later known as images, image-toys and chimney ornaments) illustrate the first attempt in the Potteries to make and sell earthenware whose sole purpose was to be decorative—like the slip-ware cat, which was usually decorated with blobs of brown slip.

In about 1700, slipware ovens continued to be packed to capacity with domestic utensils; and initially, zoomorphic figures were nothing more than a side-line for any potter wishing to pursue a novelty. Some slipware was part-functional and part-decorative, such as the owl jugs with detachable head (used as a cup) to be seen in the Greg Collection at the City Art Gallery, Manchester—the forerunner in thought for the well known salt-glazed bear-baiting jugs (Plate 228) made from about 1740.

No Staffordshire salt-glazed figures are known to be marked with the name of a potter, and only rarely are they dated (Plate 222). In common with the bulk of salt-glaze, it is quite impossible to ascribe ware to a particular manu-facturer although certain writers have, in my opinion unsuccessfully, en-deavoured to identify the work of individual potters by segregating figures on purely stylistic grounds. Perhaps the nearest we can come to factory identifi-cation is with ware bearing a pronounced similarity to Longton Hall porcelain (Plates 237 and 240) and also the lead-glazed types attributed to Thomas Whieldon (Plates 239 and 242). But it must be stressed that there is no con-crete proof which categorically links individual salt-glazed figures to either factory. Even the discovery of a salt-glazed block at Longton Hall in 1957 (Plate 38), when excavating the area in which William Littler worked, is not absolute proof that it was his product; and a small press-moulded bewigged head found on the site during 1955 (Plate 220) without doubt pre-dates the Longton porcelain venture by as much as a quarter of a century. Both Littler and Whieldon manufactured salt-glazed stoneware, amongst other products, but on neither factory-site have salt-glaze figure fragments yet been found.

An interesting lower portion of a press-moulded bird-call found in Burslem (Plate 221) belongs to the earliest period of figure-manufacture, which began in about 1725; but, unfortunately, no attribution can be given to this rarity. Similar bird-calls were being made nearly fifty years later (though not necessarily in white stoneware) according to an entry in the crate book of Thomas and John Wedgwood of the Big House, Burslem, which records their cousin Aaron Wedgwood selling to them on the 20th September 1770:

> 2 Doz Wisling Birds at 15d – 2. 6.

Another excavated figure in the City Museum, Stoke-on-Trent, is a press-moulded game-cock decorated in iron slip (Plate 219), which was found at Broughton Old Hall, Staffordshire. This specimen was also made in the Potteries in about 1725. Two similar examples can be seen in the Macy Collection, Metropolitan Museum of Art.

The few finds listed above are virtually the sum total of figure sherds unearthed in Staffordshire over the years, and no cache or kiln-wasters have ever been located. When one considers the vast quantities of white salt-glazed tavern and domestic ware which have been recovered by the spade, the obvious conclusion must be that figures formed but a relatively small proportion of the potter's output. How different from the lead-glazed earthenware figures which were mass-produced from about 1740 onwards by Astbury, Whieldon and many other Stoke-on-Trent potters. Surviving examples of this class of ware far outweigh the white salt-glazed stoneware. A rarity such as a white salt-glaze cow creamer (Plate 231), made in about 1745, becomes commonplace in its lead-glazed counterpart—particularly the multi-coloured metallic-oxide variety ascribed to Thomas Whieldon of Fenton.

Most Staffordshire salt-glazed figures were manufactured by the simple process of pressing slabs of moist clay into a two-piece mould and subsequently uniting the halves, using a slip. This technique resulted in a seam on either side of the figure which the potter attempted to remove by fettling and sponging. More often than not, the junction is still evident. It can best be seen on the interior of hollow examples, where little or no secondary work took place. A rather artless press-moulded figure of a woman wearing a wide-hooped flounced skirt with a Watteau pleat on the reverse is typical of this early type of ware, which usually lacks definition. The one illustrated in Plate 217 is in the City Museum, Stoke-on-Trent. Another example taken from the same mould is in the Victoria and Albert Museum.

A characteristic of the early hollow pieces is their primitive modelling, which is all too apparent in the standing figure (Plate 218) reputed to represent the notorious Dr. Sacheverell (1674–1724), who preached 'scandalous and seditious' sermons. (He was brought to trial in 1710 and suspended from preaching for three years. His trial was accompanied by riots and widespread agitation. It is likely that this effigy was made shortly after his death.) The game-cock already referred to (Plate 219) is another of these simple productions and here there is an affinity with the white-dipped tankard dated 1723 (Plate 58) in the use of iron slip.

An uncommon method of manufacture was the combination of throwing and hand-modelling, as shown by an unusual rattle in the Metropolitan Museum of Art (Plate 229) representing a bear hugging a dog, with details in brown slip. This unique specimen stands only two and three-quarter inches high and was made in about 1740.

What is usually considered to be the most famous class of Staffordshire figure-groups in salt-glazed stoneware is the so-called 'pew group', in which the process of press-moulding is combined with hand-modelling. Two of these amusing, original compositions form part of the Burnap Collection in the Nelson Gallery, Atkins Museum, Kansas City. One depicts a seated man and woman on a high-backed bench (Plate 225). A fearsome-looking dog separates the couple, and the man has a dog sitting between his legs. Above the perforated back is a row of six moulded faces alternating with rosettes, the detail picked out in brown clay. The other fine example (Plate 226) shows two frock-coated men playing musical instruments on either side of a woman who wears a tight bodice, and an apron over a pleated skirt. She holds a dog on her lap. The manipulative skill of the potter in arranging thin slabs of clay, press-moulded sections and hand-modelled appendages in these humorous Staffordshire pew groups is outstanding.

No less complicated in construction are the equestrian figure groups such as the greyish-white example in the City Museum, Stoke-on-Trent, of a mounted Hussar (Plate 230), which clearly indicates the complexity of press-moulding and hand-modelling. Contemporary with the pew groups (circa 1740), these rare ceramic masterpieces initiated a tradition in complicated figure groups. Within a few years, the Staffordshire potters were manufacturing horse-and-rider not only in lead-glazed earthenware decorated with polychrome metallic-oxides in the Whieldon style but also in creamware, where the colours were more subdued.

A wide variety of salt-glaze bird and animal figures originated in Staffordshire between the years 1725 and 1755, the most popular animals being dogs, cats, horses, cows, bears, deer and sheep. The majority were specifically intended as ornaments but others served a useful purpose—like the cow creamer (Plate 231), which was brought to the table filled with milk or cream. The tail acted as a handle which, when tilted, caused the contents to issue from the cow's mouth. Thoroughly unhygienic because so difficult to keep clean, but nevertheless a novelty which was to be repeated in incredible variety by a succession of potters for the next hundred and fifty years, both in earthenware and bone-china. Few salt-glaze cow creamers have survived, but by no means so rare are bear-baiting jugs with a detachable head designed for use as a cup. Shreds of clay were applied to imitate fur, and the muzzled bear is usually seen hugging a dog between its paws. In the example illustrated in Plate 228, however, the bear holds a curved whistle. Most bear-baiting jugs have dot and line detail in dark brown slip, and examples are also known in brown salt-glazed stoneware. The fashion for earthenware bear jugs continued well into the nineteenth century.

The most prolific figure in salt-glaze is, without doubt, the cat (Plates 232 and 233). It is to be found in the white, with eyes picked out in brown slip or made from bits of brown clay, or in 'solid-agate' where, by wedging different coloured clays, a marbled finish is obtained. Solid-agate cats have a white face—but where white and blue-stained clays are intermingled, the cat's ears are usually painted in cobalt. Collectors are warned of the many spurious copies which exist. Being simple to reproduce, moulds from original salt-glazed cats have been taken by forgers who, by either pressing or slip-casting, have with some degree of success imitated those first issued in about 1745. White cast examples are easy to identify because this process was never used in manufacturing the prototypes: a genuine white salt-glazed cat displays all the signs of press-moulding on the hollow interior. Solid-agate forgeries have to be press-moulded but can be detected by the poor marbling, the way in which cobalt-stained clay discolours the white, and the excessive weight. The eighteenth-century pressers were skilful artisans and their figures of cats were seldom heavy. A final word of caution: in recent years some blue and white solid-agate cats have been made in earthenware and covered with a thin smear of lead-glaze; but a forgery of this type does not show the orange-peel surface finish so characteristic of salt-glazed stoneware.

Some of the best modelling can be found on reclining horses—a favourite subject for the Staffordshire potter during the 1740s and later. A fine pair (Plate 235) in Colonial Williamsburg lie on slab-bases decorated with applied leaves and flowers. Similar examples are known in lead-glazed earthenware decorated in Whieldon-type colours.

Second only to cats in output were salt-glazed dogs (Plate 237), of which large numbers were made from about 1745. Pug-dogs sitting on rectangular slab bases are the best known. These were later manufactured in Staffordshire both in lead-glazed earthenware and porcelain. Another figure group with earthenware and porcelain counterparts is a reclining sheep and lamb, like the specimen in the Metropolitan Museum of Art (Plate 242). This particular example, based on a Chelsea porcelain original, is decorated in enamel colours. There is a similar specimen in the Victoria and Albert Museum (Schreiber Collection), and a lead-glazed example forms part of the Lucy Truman Aldrich Collection in the Rhode Island Museum of Art.

Colonial Williamsburg possesses a rare female figure made in Stoke-on-Trent in about 1735, if not earlier, which is decorated in the scratch-brown technique (Plate 223). This quaint creation is partially press-moulded, but the arms, hands, bodice and skirt are hand-modelled, with details picked out in brown clay and brown slip. Of simpler fabrication is a plain white salt-glazed Madonna and Child (Plate 227) in the City Museum, Stoke-on-Trent, inspired by a blanc-de-Chine figure of Fukien porcelain, circa 1720, depicting the Virgin Mary as Kuan Yin. This fine Staffordshire press-moulded specimen was produced around 1740. A lead-glazed coloured version is known with 'Virgin Mary' impressed on the plinth (see R. G. Haggar's, *English*

Country Pottery, Phoenix House, London, 1950, Plate 13b). Also copied from blanc-de-Chine figures of Fukien porcelain are a pair of 'Lohans' (Plate 238) which retain traces of original size-gilding. The modelling in this later class of salt-glazed product is usually of high standard.

The influence of Oriental and European porcelain figures on Staffordshire salt-glaze stoneware in the post-1740 period has long been recognised; but occasionally bronze prototypes were used, as in the case of a shepherd (Plate 239) in the City Museum, Stoke-on-Trent, made in about 1747. A companion shepherdess is known in salt-glaze, and both were manufactured in lead-glazed earthenware and Staffordshire redware. Biscuit fragments of a shepherd figure were found during excavations in Fenton Vivian on the site of a manu-factory first occupied by Thomas Whieldon in 1747. Similarities exist be-tween certain salt-glazed figures issued in the 1750s and Longton Hall porcelain. An outstanding pair of musicians in the Metropolitan Museum of Art (Plate 240) illustrate this obvious likeness, even to the crude leaf and flower ornament which decorates the base.

From about 1750, the Staffordshire potter passed to the enameller small standing figures, dancers, actors, swans and other birds to be decorated in bright colours. Some were no doubt sent to Hot Lane, Cobridge; but if William Duesbury's account book for the years 1751–3 has been interpreted correctly, a proportion were despatched to his London workshop. His des-cription of enamelling in relation to the item 'swimming swans donn all over' has been quoted many times and may refer to salt-glaze, but a more significant entry on page 5 of this important document in the British Museum reads:

9 pr of Stone Birds   10. 6
8 pr of Stone Birds   8. o

Here, the reference to 'stone' could more readily imply white salt-glazed stoneware. But not so clear is an item on page 17 of his account book which reads:

A pr of Stafordshir ladis
a pr of Stafordshir lar[ge] B[ir]ds

which could equally well refer to the enamelling of porcelain as to salt-glaze. Some fine examples of enamelled birds (Colour Plate VI) can be seen in the City Museum, Stoke-on-Trent, and a rare pair of figures decorated in polychrome enamels (Plate 243) in the Metropolitan Museum of Art.

The Burslem potters Thomas and John Wedgwood and their enlightening hitherto unpublished documents have been quoted many times in this book. It is particularly fortunate that these documents, together with a selection of the ware, should have remained in the hands of one family for two hundred years. That such an important study collection should supplement the already outstanding array of Staffordshire salt-glazed stoneware in the City Museum, Stoke-on-Trent, is entirely due to the generosity of one person, whose kindness and ready co-operation is hereby acknowledged. In this magnificent collection of salt-glazed stoneware is a unique dated specimen depicting the crucifixion (Plate 222), made either by Aaron Wedgwood or his sons Thomas and John of the Big House, Burslem, in 1732. Standing four and a quarter inches high, this press-moulded and hand-modelled example has four plain and six moulded roundels bearing unidentified coats-of-arms between which are groups of small perforations surmounted by a larger hole. For what purpose this unusual creation was intended is obscure but, irrespective of function, it remains one of the most fascinating examples of salt-glazed stoneware in existence. In a class by itself, it nevertheless forms part of one of the most successful branches of English ceramic art—one which helped to establish the Staffordshire potter in the markets of the world and, in no small measure, laid firm foundations for the great modern ceramic industry for which the City of Stoke-on-Trent is justly famous.

Appendices

Appendix I

Extracts from the Sales-Account Book of Thomas and John Wedgwood

1.

1755
Aug.ᵗ 7   Mr. Wᵐ STRAPHAN Dr. to John Wedgwood

		£ s. d.
To WSS I	} p sea	2. 15. 7
II	}	1. 16. 1
III	} Home price	2. 12. 11
IIII	}	2. 19. 1
Land Carr	}	9. 4
		10 13 0

1756
		£ s. d.
June 7	To two crates WSS I:II Kirk 8	11 13 3
Aug.ᵗ 7	To Do WSS III	5 4 0
1757 Jan 24	To pd Jackson 2/ for overweight for these two IV V	
	VI	6 17 0
Mar 12	To VII	6 2 0
Ap: 18	To	5 18 0
		35 14 3

1757
		£ s. d.
Nov. 2	To WSS I	4 9 0

P.   Contra   Cr.

1756
		£ s. d.
May 18	by Allowance	1. 3. 0
	Discount & Carr	0. 17. 6
	3 Crates Carriage before etc.	0. 11. 6
	by Cash	8. 1. 0
		10 13 0

1757
		£ s. d.
May 2	by Carr	2. 2. 6
	brokage	0. 14. 0
	Disct	1. 15. 9
	Allowᵈ	1. 2. 0
	To Draw for	30 –
	One month after 13 July have drawn to	
	Mr. Willetts for £21	–
	One month after Jan 25 1758 have drawn to	
	Miss Stringer for £9	–
1758 May 11	by Cash	3 5. 0
	Short	9. 0
	Carr broke etc	15. 0
		35 14 3
		4 9 0

2.

1755 Mr. EDWᴰ TYLSLEY Navy Office London Dr.

Sep 29 To one Crate IW ET Kirk 8/ over weight pay more 7 6 10

1756 May 12 by Cash broke & wanting .... 6. 17. 0 / 0. 9. 10 .... 7 6 10

3.

1755 Dec 6 Mr. Wm. Berrow Bristol IW WB Dr To 5 13 3

1756 Feb:16 To 6 small Fruit plates 4 6

.... 5 17 9

1756 Feb 16 By draft to Mr. R. Asbury at sight or Order allow'd .... 5. 16. 0 / 1. 9 .... 5 16 0 / 1 9

.... 5 17 9

4.

1756 Mr John Taylor Coventry Bucknall 5sc. 6lb.

June 7 To Crate 6 1 6

1757 Ap. 28 by overcharge etc. .... 0. 13. 0 / 0. 1. 0

May 26 By 3 lb Green Tea at 8/- 1. 4. 0

 1 lb Bloom Green 10 .... 0. 10. 0

 1 lb Chote 0. 4. 0

 1 lb Turkey Coffee 5. 4

 Box 8

.... 2. 18. 0 / 1. 3. 6

1758 May 19 by Tea to be sent 1. 19. 6

 by cash to his son for wine 6 1 0

5.

1760 Mr. WHITEMARSH SARUM ‡W W	Dr	£	s	d
Oct.ʳ 26 To Crate ‡W W		5	1	2½

1761	pr. Contra Cr	£	s	d
	by Abatment and Wanting	0	3	8½
	by Cash Rec.ᵈ of him	4	17	6
		5	1	2½

6.

1761 Thos Dollery Covent Garden	Dr	£	s	d
Aug.ᵗ 19 To TD I		5	13	3
1762 Feb. 15 To II		7	5	3
		12	18	6

1762	p. Contra C.ʳ	£	s	d
May 14 by Cash	0:18:0			
Note two months This p.ᵈ to Mr. Irlam	10: 0:0			
Carr. &c	2: 0:6	12	18	6

1763 Sep: 14 To Spoons in Hewson Crate		1	14	7½

1764 May 11 by Cash	1:11:6			
Allowd	3:1			
		1	14	7

7.

1762 Susanna Coward Sherborn Dorcet.ʳ		Dr.		
		£	s	d
May 1 To 2 Crates of goods ‡W SC I:II	3:16:2 / 4:15:6	8	11	8

1762	p. Contra Cr.	£	s	d
Aug.ᵗ 5	by Cash Rec.ᵈ of Mrs. Simmons Bristol	8	5	0
	by goods wanting 6s. 6d. abated 2/–		6	8
		8	11	8

8.

1762 Mr. Rich.ᵈ Asbury Sen.ʳ Bridgnorth	Dr.			
To a small crate value		2	8	9

1763 Jan.ʸ 12	by abatment	6. 9		
	by cash of him	2. 2. 6	2	8	9

9.

THOˢ. WICHELL NEWBURY Dr.		£ s d
1763 Augᵗ 26 To Crate goods ƒW TWI		7 3 9

pr. Contra Cr

1764 Augᵗ 11	by Cash Recᵈ. of him	£ 15 : 0	
	by Complaint abated	0 : 8 : 9 }	1 3 9
	by Cash Due to send a bill		
1765 July 2	by Cash p. John Poulson	6 : 0 : 0 }	6 -----
			7 3 9

10.

Wᵐ. COSBY BRISTOL Dr.		£
1763 Octʳ 14 To 1 Crate ƒW WCI		4 5 3

pr. Contra Cʳ.

| 1764 Augᵗ 6 | by abated | £0 : 4 : 3 } | |
| | by Cash Recᵈ of him | 4 : 1 : 0 } | 4 5 3 |

11.

1764 Aug 28 Samᵉˡ Pool Gloucester Dr.		
To 1 Crate ƒW SP £4. 2. 1.		4 2 1

pr. Contra

| 1765 Augᵗ 2 | by Cash Recᵈ of him | 3. 15. 0 } | |
| | by Compᵗ abated | 7. 6 } | 4 2 1 |

12.

MR. Wᵐ. HALL WINE STREET BRISTOL		
1765 Dec.ʳ 5 To Crate of goods ƒW WH		5 10 8

Pʳ. Contra

| 1766 Augᵗ 6 | by Cash Recᵈ of him | 5 : 10 : 6 } | |
| | abated | 2 } | 5 10 8 |

13.

Left (debit) side:

1765
Dec: 17   Mrs. Brougham   Newcastle upon Tine   Dr.

To   IW   WB   I: II   to the care of Benton Hull   13 17 2

1766 July 7   To   III:IV to the care of Wm. Holmes Hull   11 9 7

     25 6 9

1767
Nov: 7   To IW B Newcastle care of Wm. Sampson   7 13 8
1768 Feb: 15   To B II   Sampson   5 14 3

Note Mr. Hilcoate said Mrs. Brougham & him wd. take Mr. Gibbs two Crates 9:2:5   13 7 11

14.

James Collerick
1767 Sepr. 14   To 1 Crt IW IC   £2. 16. 8   2 16 8

Right (credit) side:

1767
Oct: 17   By Cash   22: 9: 6
Allowd   1:12: 3
Disct.   1: 5: 0
     25 6 9

1768
Sep: 30   By Cash   12:15:6
allowd   12: 5   13 7 11

1768 Mar 19   by Cash Recd of his Wife in part   2. 2. 0
1769 Aug 2   by Cash Recd. of him   9. 0. 0
Complaint   5. 8   2 16 8

Extracts from the Crate Book of Thomas and John Wedgwood

15.
             1770   Sepr. 27

Eliz Watson IW. E.W. II

8 Doz of plain Round Ta plates 2/3	18: o
6 Doz Break^st. Do. 18	9: o
2 Dishis D^o 14½ In. 15^d/4 D^o 13½ In. 12 ⎫	
4 D^o 12 In. 7½/2 D^o/10 In 4^d ⎭	9: 8
6 Washing Basons 9 In. 6 Bottles to D^o 6	6: o
8 larger 9¾In 8½	5: 8
3 two qr. jugs 8/6 three pt D^o. 6/	5: o
1 Doz qr. jugs 3 Doz pts 1 Doz Suger bouls ⎫	
o½ Doz cans & little jugs ⎭	7: 6
4½ Doz 20/	o:6: 8
	3:0:10

16.
             1771   Oct 7

Mrs Agnuss Benson Manchester

16 Picklepots	o.	1.	4
12 Do 2/ 12 D^o 4/	o.	6.	o
1 Doz Treble Starr Cups 12 ⎫			
1 Doz largest 18 ⎪			
1 Doz Starr Cups 18 ⎬	5.		o
1 Doz least puding Cups but one 12 ⎭			
2 Doz toy Teapots		1.	4
2 Doz Bowles & Basons		o.	8
5 Doz toy saucers		1.	8
6 least Fishes 10 larger 4½ 10 ⎫			
12 Double Fishes 18 ⎭		2.	6
16 Musterd pots		1.	o
3 Doz Sec^d. Cups 10^d		3.	6
2 Doz pt. & ½ pt. bouls Sec^d. 14		3.	o
6 Cham^r. Potts		3.	o
Crate		o.	10
	£1.	8.	4

17.

      1773   June 25
         W^m. Hewson

20 Groce small Gally pots	4:	o:	o
10 Groce 5	2.	10.	o
10 Groce 6	3.	o.	o

G

18.

1773		June 26		
		M^r. Wedgwood Itruria		
4	Large Puding 9		3.	0
17	Do 4		5.	8
2½	Doz double Starr petty 16		3.	4
3	Doz	12	3.	0
2½	D^o.	10	2.	1
6½	Doz Custerd 8		4.	4
6	Doz Do 10		5.	0
5½	Doz Do 12		5.	6
3½	Doz Treble Starr Cup 12		3.	6
6¼	Doz double & Treble D^o 10		5.	5
5	Doz double & Treble D^o 8		3.	4
12	Doz Custerd Cups 8⎫		0. 11.	0
12	Doz Do 10⎭		~~0. 12. 0~~	
14	Doz Pap spoons 10		0. 11.	8
12	Doz large Tea Spoons		8.	0
4½⎫	⎱Doz Custerd 12 10		4.	6
4 ⎭			3.	4
2	Doz large double petty 16		2.	8
3	Doz midle	12	3.	0
1½	Doz least	10	1.	3
3	Doz Treble Starr Cup large 12		3.	0
6	Doz Treble & double	10	5.	0
4½	Doz least D^o	8	2.	6
			5. 0.	1

Note:

In quoting from the sales-account book, it cannot be absolutely certain that all sales refer to salt-glaze because no breakdown of the crate-contents is given.

The only surviving crate-book compiled by the Wedgwood brothers covers the period 1770–73. Though care has been taken to exclude accounts which mention the sale of creamware, redware etc., there can be no guarantee that every item quoted above relates to salt-glaze, although Thomas and John Wedgwood were the largest manufacturers of salt-glazed stoneware in Burslem.

British and American Museums where Staffordshire Salt-glazed Stoneware is represented

Public Museums: England

Bedford: Cecil Higgins Museum
Brighton: Museum & Art Gallery
Cambridge: Fitzwilliam Museum
Leeds: Temple Newsam House
Liverpool: City Museum
London: British Museum
London: Victoria & Albert Museum
Manchester: City Art Gallery
Nottingham: City Museum
Preston: Harris Museum & Art Gallery
Sheffield: City Museum
Stoke-on-Trent: City Museum

Public Museums: America

Boston: Museum of Fine Arts
Cambridge: Fogg Museum of Art
Charlotte: Mint Museum (Delhom Gallery)
Chicago: Art Institute
Cleveland: Museum of Art
Colonial Williamsburg
Dearborn: Henry Ford Museum
Kansas City: Nelson Gallery—Atkins Museum
New York: Metropolitan Museum of Art
Philadelphia: Museum of Art
Washington: Smithsonian Institute
Winterthur: Henry Francis du Pont Museum

Bibliography

Barber, Edwin Atlee. *Salt Glazed Stoneware*. London. Hodder & Stoughton. 1907 (Primers of industrial art).

Bimson, Mavis. John Dwight. *English Ceramic Circle Transactions*. Vol. 5. Part 2. 1961. pp. 95–109.

Blacker, J. F. *The A.B.C. of English Salt-glaze Stoneware from Dwight to Doulton*. London, Stanley Paul. 1922.

Boney, Dr. Knowles. 'Study of a Group of English Salt-glaze ware', *Antiques*. December, 1965. pp. 834–7.

Caddie, Alfred J. 'Some Rare Specimens of Staffordshire Salt-Glazed Ware', *Connoisseur*. Vol. 16. 1906. pp. 216–18.

Church, A. H. *Some Minor Arts as Practised in England*. London, Seeley & Co. 1894. Old English Pottery. pp. 27–46.

Cook, Cyril. 'Old English Salt-Glazed Plates with Printed Decorations' *Connoisseur*. Antique Dealers Fair and Exhibition Number, 1958. pp. 39–43.

Cushion, John P. 'Ceramics for Collector and Potter. No. 4. Salt-glazed stoneware.' *Studio*. Vol. 160. November 1960. pp. 182–3.

Drinkwater, John. 'Some Notes on English Salt-Glaze Brown Stoneware', *English Ceramic Circle Transactions*. Vol. II. 1939. No. 6. pp. 31–9.

Freeth, Frank. 'Old English Saltglaze Tea-pots', *Connoisseur*. Vol. 5. 1903. pp. 108–15.

Haggar, Reginald G. 'Two Salt glazed Primitives', *Apollo*. Vol. 48. 1948. pp. 118–19.

Hemming, Celia. 'On Staffordshire Salt-glaze', *Connoisseur*. Vol. 47. 1917. pp. 208–17.

Hobson, R. L. 'Early Staffordshire Wares Illustrated by Pieces in the British Museum'. *Burlington Magazine*. Vol. 4. 1904. Part IV 'Salt-glazed ware', pp. 148–54.

— 'New Acquisitions in the British Museum. The Harland Saltglaze', *Burlington Magazine*. Vol. 37. 1920. pp. 83–4.

Honey, W. B. 'English Saltglazed Stoneware', *English Ceramic Circle Transactions*. Vol. 1. No. 1. 1933. pp. 12–22.

* Hume, Ivor Noël. 'Mugs, Jugs and Chamber Pots' [A note enlarging and discussing an article by Knowles Boney: 'Study of a Group of English Salt-Glaze Ware'.] *Antiques*. October, 1966. pp. 520–2.

— 'The Rise and Fall of English White Salt-glazed Stoneware', *Antiques*. Part I, February, 1970, pp. 248–55. Part II, March, 1970. pp. 408–13.

Luxmoore, Charles, F. C. *Saltglaze; with the Notes of a Collector*. Exeter. Wm. Pollard. 1924.

Rackham, Bernard. 'A Dated Staffordshire Mug in National Museum of Wales, Cardiff', *English Ceramic Circle Transactions*. Vol. II. No. 8. pp. 145–8.

Read, Herbert. 'Staffordshire Salt-Glaze in the Collection of Mr. J. Henry Griffith'. Part I. *Connoisseur*. Vol. 70. 1924. pp. 193–202.

— 'Staffordshire Salt-Glaze in the Collection of Mr. J. Henry Griffith'. Part II. *Connoisseur*. Vol. 71. 1925. pp. 25–30.
— 'Staffordshire Salt-Glaze in the Collection of Mr. J. Henry Griffith'. Part III. *Connoisseur*. Vol. 71. 1925. pp. 81–7.
Rhead, G. Woolliscroft. 'More about Salt Glaze'. *Connoisseur*. Vol. 26. 1910. pp. 30–2.
Solon, M. L. *Salt glaze;* the catalogue of a small collection now exhibited in the Technical Museum at Hanley, to which has been prefixed a disquisition on salt glaze ware by the collector. Hanley. 1890.
Taggart, Ross. 'How to Identify Wedgwood Salt Glaze', *Minutes of the Third Wedgwood International Seminar 1958*. pp. 85–9.
Tait, Hugh. ' "Blocks" for Spouts', *British Museum Quarterly*. Spring 1963. p. 103.
Turner, William. 'Crouch Ware'. Part I. *Connoisseur*. Vol. 11. 1905. pp. 43–9.
— 'Crouch Ware'. Part II. *Connoisseur*. Vol. 13. 1905. pp. 96–102.
— 'A Group of Old Salt-glaze', *Connoisseur*. Vol. 39. 1914. pp. 194–5.
— 'Salt-glazed Ware', *Ceramics*. June, 1953. pp. 162–5.

Index

(Does not include lists of Staffordshire potters to be found on pages 14–16 and 19)